pjoriley

Atheist in Church
on Heaven and Other Mysteries

Pjoriley Wordworks
http://www.pjoriley.com
ISBN 0615629342 / 978-0615629346

Cover design by KC Berger
Text font - Constantia

Contents

Atheist in Church

The believer is happy, the doubter is wise.
Irish proverb

DP —
You're the Best!

Paula
Pigo

1

Introduction
Why Church, Why Now?

I t's not all that hard to be an atheist. You don't
have to dress up and go somewhere for worship.
There's no pressure to tithe or sing in the choir,
and no need to debate the merits of one religious text
versus another. No faith-based embarrassment at the
peccadilloes or fraud perpetrated by a church official.
There is less to memorize, and fewer rules. You need not
assess a political candidate's religious bent, except, perhaps, to exclude the occasional radical. And this may
seem a small thing, but none of the common, useful
swear words are off limits to atheists. Sure, there will be
times when an employer, friend, or acquaintance will
turn you away for lack of God-belief, but otherwise,
atheism is easy as pie, *if* you don't mind being a disbeliever in a largely believing culture.

About disbelieving: it's relatively painless to ignore
believers, in spite of how often they make the news with
theological pronouncements or bloody confrontations.
Even when they offer up a bit of scripture as explanation
for an otherwise natural occurrence, a person can smile
and nod at someone else's perspective; no need to offer
an alternate view. And an atheist need not examine why

they themselves don't believe in God or gods. They can easily remain indifferent, like I did, until an opportunity presents itself and they cannot help peering harder than usual at the well of belief that surrounds them every day (I want to know about most things, even if I don't subscribe to them. Plus, I'm not convinced that what we don't know can't hurt us; the opposite seems more likely to be true.).

I was raised by a Christian mother and a nonbelieving father in a family where our mother, the first line of parental authority, shepherded us to church every Sunday. But sitting weekly in a church, even one with stained glass windows and polished hardwood pews, didn't convince me of the teachings. As the choir sang and the reverend preached, other places called to me: my single bed with its chenille coverlet, our backyard of shade trees and Shepherd dog, the basketball game in the neighbor's driveway. Still, the choice was mine: church versus certain punishment for disobedience (lectures, grounding). Ever the pragmatist, I climbed aboard the boat headed to church.

The memoir you are reading started as research for a novel in which my protagonist, based on a historical figure, has knowledge of Jewish and certain Christian practices. My childhood experiences taught me enough to be, as they say, dangerous, but not enough to render my chosen character and her circumstances believable. That is why I set out to visit Foursquare Gospel, Christian Science, Catholic, and Jewish services. Those few specific theologies would do the job; no more, no less. And since Heaven is a component of my novel's narrative, I meant to engage people in conversation about their notions regarding the hereafter.

I was fairly certain that I might be the only atheist attending synagogue. There might be agnostics in a church crowd, a few skeptics, and seekers galore. I would bet my laptop, though, that on any given worship day you would not find the back pockets of bona fide disbelievers polishing the pews. That's because few atheists can conjure reasons to visit a church or synagogue, thinking that nothing therein—the music, the people, the communities themselves—could fuel their thoughts in a productive manner. Two years ago I may have held those same notions, and to be frank, it was simpler and easier not to expend much energy considering the folks who play for God's team. I thought I knew enough about why I don't believe in God. As it turns out, I was wrong.

Some atheists, a vocal minority, describe believers as delusional. Even if that term were technically accurate for people believing in and praying to an invisible, mute spirit-entity, it falls harshly on my ears. I am like so many of the largely silent majority of non-believers who shake their heads and marvel at the irregularities in the behavior of people who otherwise strike us as level-headed, while seeing no reason to call them names. When believers claim they are the only right thinkers, they sound, well, irrational, because who among them can prove the existence of God, or disprove God's non-existence? They cannot. Conversely, why would any atheist think that diatribes or polemics would work to dispel God-belief, when science has clearly failed?

Atheists ranting against believers and believers preaching that atheists have it all wrong are wasting time and energy. The only people granting credence to such rhetoric have probably already bought in on one side or the other, where they intend to stand firm. I am not trying to change anyone's mind, to convince any believer to switch sides. I am simply interested in the nature of God-belief and why it seems the perfect fit for so many others, but not for me.

Back to my research: If you imagine that disbelievers would turn to believing if only they received the proper explications, the right teacher, or a full and heartfelt church experience, you are likely wrong. Religion has been such a staple of American life that a majority of my generation and earlier received adequate enough religious exposure for us to either sign up or opt out. Such is my recollection of how church services work that if I wanted, I could emulate the sincere participation of Christian believers. I could easily have blended in while making the rounds through the churches on my list. I could have blended in, but I meant to leave no trail of false impressions. Here then was my plan: I would go from church to synagogue as a casual visitor, observing as unobtrusively as possible. I would stand when a congregation stood, listen intently, and keep time to the music without singing. No one would mistake me for someone seeking a new church home.

For decades I have managed to sidestep organized religion through a kind of benign avoidance, the way I might look the other way when the busboy comes by with a pitcher of tea. In addition to having had my fill, I am engaged in conversation with my lunch date. Got enough, thanks, no more, *no more* or I might float away.

In the last few years, though, my radar attuned itself to various reports about the religious bent of Americans, and to certain books, articles, interviews, and documentaries. Religion and God-belief became one of those backcountry radio frequencies that bleeds into other programs. Between snatches of whichever NPR station shows up on the repeater, comes a Christian radio station broadcasting prayers and sermons and gospel music. In my book that's not divine intervention, but the inevitable commerce of religion. Voyeur that I am, I started to tune in. I clipped stories and dog-eared the pages of books. I was working on my second novel at the time and found such distractions welcome during my slog through a long project.

Without me intending it so, those distractions turned into a deeper interest: all those believers and each one holding his or her personal beliefs face-up toward the sun, refracting bits of light and color across the space surrounding us all, even the square on which I stood. I stepped closer, and guess what? I now own two or three sets of lectures by professors and other scholars on subjects such as comparative religion and the making of the Biblical canon.

While there is plenty to be admired in people of faith, I cannot abide the dogma of organized religion. During those long-ago mornings in church with my mother and brothers, Bible stories sounded like fiction. Interesting, exotic fiction, woven with strong language, obviously much admired but marked by implausible versions of creation and a certain endgame. Another thing: I could not fathom why so many people were ardent followers while I seemed incapable of God-belief. I just couldn't buy in, but while I found God-belief illogical, even fanciful, I have never thought of believers as crazy. Of the things I knew then and find as true today, one is that the spectrum of humanity is vast, encompassing many thoughts and behaviors that for various reasons I don't practice (some of them I probably should).

Then there's the matter of Heaven, which I needed to construct for my novel. Though I found good material in Lisa Miller's book titled *HEAVEN—OUR ENDURING FAS-CINATION WITH THE AFTERLIFE*, I wanted to personally gather other people's ideas and insights. And too, I like to gab—as long as other people do most of the talking. Though I can fictionalize a variety of potential Heavens, work best left until after sufficient digging and many gentle inquiries, I am captivated by looking a person in the eye and hearing them speak of pearled gates or the expectation of a spirit world to which all people pass. Through this method I've collected and considered the perspectives of others, believers and non-, each of which sent my thoughts bumping along, leading to the effort on these pages.

Eventually my narrow quest broadened as I began to contemplate the differences in how people worship and what they say about faith and Heaven. Thoughts about God-belief trailed me through my days, even when I wasn't sitting through a church service or interviewing someone. At one point I even considered sampling each religion and denomination listed in our community's phone directory. You'll see that I didn't get that far.

I am not a scholar of world religions. I don't even study religion, per se, other than I am a studier of people, and religion plays such an integral part in many people's lives. My research began with a specific agenda, but, as can happen, it led me down additional paths. Credit my affinity for tangents, those ephemeral strings that lead not from point A to B, but arc instead toward some other point situated along a less-traveled road, or else one that leads to nowhere. So it was that I took a few detours, and wouldn't you know it, arrived at a wayside both inspired and inspiring.

My forays took place in my home of forty years: Reno, Nevada, cupped in a high desert valley ringed by snow-catching, sun-splashed mountains. Reno possesses the same penchant for gambling games and booze as does Las Vegas, while remaining less garish and much prettier. And of course there's more to Reno (and its sister-city, Sparks) than apparent at first glance: industry and entrepreneurship, a lively cultural scene, a white water park in the center of downtown, triple-A baseball, an expanding University system, bike paths, hiking trails. I could go on, but I'll spare you.

Our metro area sits in what's called the Truckee Meadows, which contains roughly 350,000 residents. At my count there are approximately 170 churches, temples, synagogues, and mosques, a number that has surely grown with the area's expanding population, especially the last twenty years or so. Each one might serve one or two hundred worshipers per week, some surely draw three-to-five hundred. That means that on any given day, roughly 10% of all local residents attend a service, some being weekly worshipers, others making less frequent appearances. If the regulars are half the total and other half are monthly-goers, perhaps 30% of locals attend church at least once a month. One hundred seventy worship houses sounds like a lot to me, but believers might think it on the thin side. Certainly those 170 mean to answer residents' appetite for religion and their desire for choice in worship.

It seems that everywhere I look there are articles and references to the current state of religion in America, how religion shapes politics, or how faith has saved someone's life. When so many others within my culture hold dear a set of beliefs that are clearly contrary to my own, I cannot help but be fascinated by both the variety and disparity of competing religious and anti-religious messages. The public debate over God-belief looms large and personal, and as it already constitutes a fair portion of the world's attention and enmity, I can only imagine it challenging people's relations with each other for generations to come.

Speaking of God-belief, I use the terms *belief* or *believing* as shorthand for God-belief. I also use the term God, though readers may favor Allah or Jehovah or Yahweh. For simplicity sake I use God to mean either God in the Christian sense, or the Old Testament sense, or else a God-like creator, all-knowing, all-seeing, all everything (and I don't mean Rush Limbaugh, who at one time in his radio promos referred to himself with a similar string of superlatives). So, God it is. You can insert your preference where appropriate and know that my distillation means no disrespect.

I regularly talk religion and philosophy with Lisa M, author, high school teacher, and former Catholic who has extensive personal and acquired knowledge of the Catholic Church's evolution over time. She sounds cynical when we discuss the Bible's male-centric narrative and Christianity's denigration of women. Few things ruffle her as do the "inventions of the Old Testament" and the misogyny of Muslim, Jewish, and Christian teachings, which scapegoat women in order to justify the patriarchal power agenda. The change in her is subtle, but I can tell when she's steamed. Our exchanges include our respective interpretations of the variations of Christianity, the construction of belief systems, and topics like myth, transcendence, and humanism; these sessions have influenced me to think more deeply.

My consumption of articles and books, blogs, commentaries, and documentaries about religion also finds reflection within these pages, along with direct quotes from generous individuals who spoke with me about their personal histories, their beliefs, and their questions relating to faith.

I have done my best to accurately quote individuals whose beliefs illustrate the breadth of religious and spiritual diversity found in my own personal universe. While the majority of this manuscript represents my own musings, at the end of the day, it simply would not exist without the generosity of others.

More about fiction: Even if characters are entirely made up, including their motivations and their backstories and such, the concrete details of their lives must be formed from clay resembling that found in real life, enough so that a reader enjoins the fiction and finds herself in the scene with the characters. If a writer does not possess sufficient life experience to serve as a story's bricks and mortar, twigs or straw, said materials must be gathered through some sort of research, primary sources being best. So it was that I set out to soak up the particulars which will allow my novel's protagonist to come alive on the page. There you have it: my reasons for this atheist to attend church.

2

Skeptics and Believers

A ttending church as a non-believer rekindled certain long-buried sensations, particularly the employment of a carefully constructed facade for gaining entrance where the normal self, the real self, held no currency with the bouncer at the door. No proper credentials, no PASS GO card. You can dress the part and talk a good game, but at the end of the day you're still a poser at someone else's party. They know it, and you know it, and sometimes they know you know it.

I made a plan to visit worship places in the most benign way possible, to sample how they look and sound, and the taste of them in my mouth. Though unconcerned that an hour here and another there would alter my thoughts about how the universe appears to clasp us in its starry grip, a part of me imagined that an inspired and passionate sermon might prove revelatory after all: Aha, there *is* a God. I did not expect such a discovery, but hey, things happen.

At about the time I began my rounds I read a biography of Abraham Lincoln written by Stephen B. Oates. In it, Lincoln's correspondence and the scrupulously kept records of his conversations with all manner of advisors and confidants reveal him as a skeptic about organized religion.

This gave me heart because here was a man facing serious challenges, both individually and on behalf of a divided nation, a country on the brink of a bloody civil war, yet he didn't look only outward, or upward. He leapt to no assumption that war was God's wish, as others of his day might have. Instead he looked to the country's culture, to the advice of many advisors, and inward to his own considerable intellect and reasoning, eventually making a series of decisions to steer the country away from the manmade, Bible-condoned practice of slavery. Eventually he led the North in waging war on Southern secessionists while the country held a clotted rag to the wounds of its divergent ideologies.

How easy it would have been to capitulate to the many who asserted that God had designated European-born whites as superior to African slaves. Even if Lincoln hadn't been a cautious thinker and master of compromise (also a doting father), I would admire how he avoided the religious quicksand of his era, choosing to champion broad human rights over the self-service of narrower thinking.

Lincoln was a believer of sorts. He prayed and on occasion used God-language. It served him politically, socially, and personally not to be an atheist, but skepticism suited him.

Ever since the first settlers came to our country's shores, our culture has plugged its nose and held itself at a distance from atheism. In 2010, polls put the number of American disbelievers in the low double digits, roughly the same percentage as for gays and lesbians.

On the west coast, where I've lived all my life, it's uncommon for people to ask about religious or spiritual practices unless the conversational context invites inquiry. People might ask about the kind of work you do or what part of town you live in, did you watch the Super Bowl, and Hey, how about those Giants? Disbelief doesn't seem to offend people, but it is often tucked away. Only close friends know that it sleeps under the bed with dust bunnies. Or maybe I'm being cynical, since west coast attitudes do seem to allow for nonconformity.

There was a time in America when almost everyone belonged to a church, whether true believer or not. The majority were members of Christian churches, especially Protestant, but in any case God-believing. Nonmembership signaled a person who could not be trusted, someone dissociated from the common good, possessor of low morals and questionable judgment, given to bucking the crowd. At best, unseemly, and probably a bit *off*. At worst, a heretic, fodder for the stockades, dunking, or burning. Pious times, those, but no more. I find that though many people today believe in a creator, questions about religious affiliation are not top of mind, and lack of religious affiliation no longer casts a shadow over someone to be feared or shunned. Still, there remains a whiff of the remarkable about atheism, when in fact it might well be as ordinary as milk.

For an on-line community art project called "PostSecret," Frank Warren solicited people's secrets about love, fear, hope, or anything they wanted to share anonymously. The submissions came by internet and on handwritten postcards, others on typed pages, here and there a personal photo tucked in. Stories suspended whole within the prism of a single sentence, pocket-sized riffs encompassing the world. I picture the earth's poles flexing at the release of all those closely held narratives, gravity adjusting for a tiny extra spring in so many people's steps.

Warren ended up publishing these bits in book form, too, with one of the volumes titled *A Lifetime of Secrets*. You've seen those "six word novels" that shave a plot down to the story equivalent of thong underwear. Similar animals, these, only perhaps they'd be cotton briefs. One I have copied out reads: *I've been an atheist for years but sometimes I miss church. Tell your God I said, 'Hi.'*

The way writers will do, I exchanged portions of this manuscript with other writers for feedback on content, tone, pacing, transitions, all manner of writing elements. About thirty pages in, one of them said, "Reading this makes me want to ask how you became an atheist." Her comment gives me leave to answer here what there was no time then to explain. This may be a matter of semantics and I may be misinterpreting her feedback. I took her to be referencing not only my lack of God-belief, but my lack of any religious or spiritual bent. My answer goes like this: I don't believe a person *becomes* an atheist any more than they become a female, or a natural brunette. They are born to it.

My paternal grandmother, Hazel, had a penchant for Siamese cats, especially those with six toes, that extra toe being a rarity. Her cats, one of whom she named Piewacket (or, perhaps Pyewacket, for a cat in a 1958 romantic comedy), could not have grown only five toes instead of six. It's the way he arrived on this planet.

What happens to distinguish atheists from believers is that atheists remain as they came out blinking into the light of day—non-religious. Neither Christians nor

Muslims, Hindus or Buddhists are born with religion swimming their blood any more than they're born knowing how to shoot hoops, till the garden, play an instrument, or fly a kite.

For years I've maintained the point of view that religion is learned from others, an example of nurture versus nature, a cultural construct containing history and promise, but a human construct nonetheless. I'm sure people gravitate to religion to answer questions about themselves, the larger world, and whether there's an afterlife. But it isn't like having six toes. Parents and the larger culture surrounding each of us cultivate pathways leading to religion. That's why in one part of the world people worship Yahweh and in another they worship rain gods.

If God were inborn, humans would all worship the same supernatural entity no matter their native language, no matter their pedigree or heritage or race, without anyone else pointing the way. From the moment they could think, they would believe. And yet they don't. Some believe in different versions of God or various prophets and seers, others in witchcraft and Satan. Still others don't believe in any supernatural being at all.

Atheists are not born believers to later somehow fall into an abyss of non-believing. As humans we can be shaped by the beliefs of other people who came before us—parents, teachers, priests—or of our own accord seek transcendence or spiritual experiences, but with that first squalling breath, we are born atheists.

3
First Sunday

~~Potter's House Christian Fellowship~~

On a warm fall Sunday I attended Potter's House Christian Fellowship for what would be roughly my fourth church service in thirty-five years. I chose Potter's House by perusing the phone book. You might think: The phone book? Such ancient technology! Well, churches have ancient roots, so there. And of course, it worked. I found a directory listing for a church led by two *evangelists*. My New Oxford American Dictionary defines evangelist as: a person who seeks to convert others to the Christian faith, especially one who does so by public preaching.

Potter's House resides in an unprepossessing industrial district in east Reno. Over the decades, modern churches have sprung up in all manner of locations: strip malls, bookstores, private homes, former service stations. They can be found as single-purpose structures, as in my youth they all were, but more and more they might be multi-purpose spaces or else share a business complex with other enterprises. Some are even in shopping malls. Mega-churches and televangelist operations are the vocal, visible few. More numerous are community and neighborhood churches, often of the organic variety, springing up wherever the hunger is greatest, starting on a shoestring and fed by their members' appetites for connection, community, and a pathway to the metaphysical.

The entry doors of Potter's House open onto a wide foyer leading in one direction to offices and small meeting spaces, and in the other direction to a large auditorium for communal Bible study and worship. Just inside the door I was greeted by a man who asked my name. He gave his as Landon. He looked to be in his early thirties.

The thing about being a newbie at church is that it's hard to blend in. Church leaders and regular members easily recognize each other and can spot the newcomer at first glance. A slight hesitation upon entering gives you away. It's like my friend Lisa says about hearing non-native French speakers in conversation. They can be quite good but there is an almost imperceptible stutter in phrasing as the brain sifts through options and how to parse them. For the speaker there's an unintended observation of the speech process and a tad too much precision because it's not automatic. That was me in church, non-automatic.

I identified myself as a visitor. Landon welcomed me and offered a schedule of weekly worship services, Bible studies, and witnessing sessions. Having arrived a bit early for Sunday service, I sat in on the last half-hour of Bible Study already under way. It was led by a middle-aged, dark-haired man dressed in a dark suit. He stood at a lectern on the central podium, discussing Bible teachings with the assemblage of two or three dozen people. Helpers brought a microphone to those who replied to the questions posed about morals and how to bring God into their lives.

The evangelist, named Lewis, was articulate and as-
sertive, each of his questions flowing smoothly into the
next, each bit of scripture leading to an explanation of
its application to modern life. He called upon people by
name. Thinking back, I observed only men answering
the calls for response, though there were plenty of
women present. Alongside adults sitting two rows ahead
of me, a couple of teenagers slouched in their chairs as if
they'd rather be somewhere else.

The meeting space was large, could easily seat three
hundred. More people arrived as the Bible Study concluded, eventually numbering almost one hundred for
the service, all different ages: mostly Latinos and Cauca-
sians, two African-Americans, and two of Asian descent.
The formality of dress closely resembled the church-
going days of my youth, with women in skirts or dresses,
men in slacks, pastors in suits.

So often you see crosses in traditional Christian
churches. No cross or artwork bearing that symbol
adorned any of the walls of this meeting space. Here the
colors were muted and soft, the walls without windows.

An aside I'll make here about churches will illuminate one of my personal biases. It seems that when a
church has no windows, a certain connection to the outside world is lost. No way to enjoy the morning's glow or
the shift of light as noon draws near. No musings about
the weather, either, no spring fever, and no one need
wield a squeegee. I know, *I know*, a person should be
able to pray anywhere, worship anywhere, without ban-
ners or alters or icons or windows. I care nothing for
icons, but the lack of windows—*that* seemed a disappointment. Must be my penchant for fresh air and birdsong. While I'm inside, the glimpse, the mere hint at

what lies outdoors is enough to satisfy me (I am that way about restaurants too; don't want to feel corralled).

The spare look of Potter's House contrasts with the more elaborate, cross-shaped church of my youth, full of dark wood and stained-glass windows. But perhaps to this congregation, aesthetic features and traditional comforts are less important than a focus on worship. After all, faith itself doesn't require fancy pews and costly accouterments. Plus, the cost of operating a church must be considerable, especially from the year 2000 forward, when the Reno area saw double-digit growth and steady increases in property values. After the financial collapse of 2008, property values and leasing costs plummeted while people lost jobs, income, and savings. Even without a stand-alone structure, a church's operating costs could be considerable. For Potter's House I can list some potential expenses: rent and maintenance, utilities, office supplies, printing, three hundred padded chairs, a sound system. Running a church takes money.

Landon had handed me a glossy postcard for Saturday's upcoming "Anti-A" gathering, a music party for young people with all ages welcome. I didn't tumble to the capital A. Alcohol? Adultery? Seeing the puzzled look on my face he explained the abbreviation as "Anti-Atheist." I thought to myself: Little does he know.

Another handout listed a weekly "New Converts Class," Spanish-language Bible Study, Sunday school for children, and a drama group. On the front of the handout, this passage from Proverbs: "Trust in the Lord with all thine heart; and lean not unto thine own understanding. In all thy ways acknowledge him, and he shall direct thy paths. (Proverbs 3:5-6)" There is also a weeknight service that includes "witnessing," which is where members share their experiences of finding God, accepting Jesus as their savior, and reporting how God has answered their prayers.

Music, a universal element in worship services, formed a majority of the service, which was led by an evangelist named Mike. I wasn't bold enough to take notes during this, my first research outing, but my recollections immediately afterward included Mike's reference to mankind being made "not in the physical image of God," but "in the image of his spirit." I had to wonder if that meant that all people are cast from God's spirit, even the Muslims, Buddhists, Hindus, Jews, even the non-believers. Wouldn't that mean that all belief systems, diverse as they are, spring from the same spirit? Aren't they all then of equal veracity, all valuable? Aren't they all blessed and holy?

One thing about evangelists, they sound certain that Biblical teachings are *right*, which gives them an aura of conviction. Good thing, as it must take conviction to get big things done, like building up a church. Then again, an unwavering certainty about being right, knowing the "one true path" seems close kin to the type of certitude that drives extremists of any faith to crusade against others who believe differently, others deemed *wrong*. It seems to me that if people were more flexible about the attributes of right living, we might build a less hostile, more cooperative world. Instead of facing off against them, we'd more often stand beside our brothers and sisters, the better to see value in their diverse views.

A group of musicians ascended the Potter's House platform: a guitarist-vocalist, a keyboard player, two women vocalists, and a drummer who sat behind a clear plastic panel. The songs they played were not the traditional hymns from my youth, the ones arranged for organ accompaniment or exaltation by choirs. These contained simple melodic hooks and reverential lyrics. According to Diane Ackerman, author of *A Natural History of the Senses*, when people sing their endorphin levels rise and their pupils dilate. That might be why worshipers report feeling uplifted by song, and why so many of us sing in the car or shower (well, there are those great acoustics).

The Potter's House congregation stood to sing, clapping their hands and swaying to the beat. There were no hymnals or song sheets. The lyrics appeared on a large screen at the front, and one of the songs made reference to Mexico.

Following the sermon there was a call for prayers while helpers passed collection baskets. Worshippers came forward to kneel on the steps of the podium. Others came forward, too, stopping alongside those who knelt, for each petitioner, a partner. I imagined each prayer partner boosting the other person's prayer upon his shoulders, lifting it a little closer to God. The music played on.

There would surely have been some mingling and conversation after the service, but I had not yet prepared a satisfactory explanation for my interest, so I exited promptly, carrying the handouts I'd been given, one of which reads, "Find Hope for your life through Jesus Christ. Marriages Restored — Deliverance from Addictions — Miracle Healing — Preaching the 'uncut' Word of God."

I admit that I virtually held my breath during that service, observing the attentiveness of worshippers around me while simultaneously expecting someone to peg me as imposter. I am sure that some congregants noted my silence during songs and prayers, though they might have approved my contribution to the collection plate. I suspect I did not appear engaged, did not look the part of seeker (How might a seeker look?). They had welcomed me into their house of worship and not turned me out for lack of enthusiasm. Inside me burned a glimmer of gratitude. The first leg of my journey complete, I stepped out into the light blue heat of a high desert September, got into my car, and drove away.

~~ Hillside Foursquare Church ~~

That first visit to Potter's House had gone well enough that I soon visited another church on my list—Hillside Foursquare Church. Foursquare is a type of evangelical church. As explained in one of the church's handouts, Foursquare stands for Jesus Christ, The Savior; Jesus Christ, The Baptizer with the Holy Spirit; Jesus Christ, The Healer; and Jesus Christ, The Soon-Coming King.

The church was founded by Aimee Semple McPherson, who is reported to have preached in 1922 to a crowd of eight thousand in Oakland, California. Her preaching included lessons and descriptions from Ezekiel 1:4-10, which provided a prophet's vision of four creatures with the faces of a man, lion, ox, and eagle. For her Foursquare theology, McPherson developed the theological symbols of a cross, a dove, a cup, and a crown.

Hillside's church resembles a modern cement fortress at the northern end of the city, situated on a high point of a hill that was once the outskirts of town. When first constructed the church probably stood alone among the sagebrush and scrub with just a paved road leading to it from the wide boulevard below. Now other businesses and a condominium complex dot the nearby landscape, but Hillside commands the ultimate top spot.

Just inside its glass entryway a friendly fair-haired woman greeted me. She wore jeans and a casual top. A nametag identified her as Joni. When I mentioned the informal atmosphere, Joni said that its purpose was to make everyone feel welcome no matter how they dressed. I explained my mission. She commended my plan to visit a variety of churches, perhaps many of those represented around town, and expressed an interest in reading what I wrote about Hillside.

The sugar junkie in me snapped to attention at the luscious fog of aromas drifting from the main worship hall. I stepped closer to discover fresh-baked cookies, brownies, and scones piled high on tables to my right, and opposite, a full coffee set-up. Like a delicious dream, better than buttered popcorn at the cinema, better even than a coffee shop, because here the sugared air perfumed every inch. The place smelled as inviting as a mother's warm kitchen with cookies fresh from the oven. Even for people without a mother who plied such magic, it embodied the essence of coming home. I felt the urge to linger a while.

In his book titled *Buy-ology—Truth and Lies About Why We Buy*, Martin Lindstrom, a marketing and branding professional, explains *neuromarketing*, which he calls "an intriguing marriage of marketing and science." In a lengthy study he helped plan and orchestrate, scientists used functional magnetic resonance imagining (fMRI) to examine the brains of participants being presented with various products, images, and cigarette package warnings.

The purpose was to better understand the psychology of why consumers purchase one product versus another. Because modern science knows which areas of the brain "light up" with neural activity for various conscious and unconscious processes, brain responses to purposefully applied stimuli can be measured in real time, yielding general deductions about positive (happy) or negative (including fearful) brain activity. So says Mr. Lindstrom.

He deduces that people verbalize preferences which are often quite different (sometimes opposite) from what their brain activity reveals. As well, he asserts that positive associations carry emotional weight, writing "...emotions are the way in which our brains code things of value." His business pertains to consumer products and brands, but when it comes to our brains assigning value to things, would not that same emotional coding apply to religious choices and beliefs?

Lindstrom also asserts that the more people feel anxious and uncertain, the more they adopt ritual and superstitious practices. Science has linked superstition and ritual to "humans' need for control in a turbulent world." Furthermore, he identifies what scientist Antonio Damasio calls "somatic markers," the sum of physical, emotional, and intellectual experiences that create a type of cognitive shortcut between a received stimulus and an appropriate reaction that will point us toward the least painful outcome.

According to Lindstrom we make dozens, maybe hundreds, of choices each day based on these shortcuts, some of the strongest being those made from fear of social ills such as being thought old or ugly or unsuccessful. Some fears are grounded in vanity, some in a drive to amass material wealth or spiritual fulfillment. In fact, he asserts that fear-based messages are the ones most forcefully received by our brains, and that is why we act upon them. It's that old treadmill of "If I don't do that/ buy that/ look like that" others will perceive me a failure.

He doesn't say it but I will: Isn't there a fear-factor inherent in the contemplation of failing to meet God's favor? Or in how right-living could lead to Heaven and wrong-living to Hell? There's that ancient yet modern fear about this one life being all there is. And shouldn't a person choose in favor of Heaven and God, you know, in case he *does* exist? because you'd hate to get to the end and find out that you should have believed all along.

More marketing insights that Lindstrom learned from his very expensive study (underwritten by international corporate sponsors): Sight is very nearly the least useful of our senses when it comes to the creation of compelling somatic markers. Touch, sound and scents make for the most arresting memories, as long as they logically, pleasingly match the visual cues on offer.

A confession: I have a terrible memory for the plots of most books and movies I've enjoyed, and a worse memory for characters and the actors who play them. My Achilles heel: proper names and place names. But I will never *ever* forget the sensory experience of visiting Hillside Foursquare Church. I don't know whether the church's leaders know or intuit the science underlying how their worship environment works on congregants, or whether they simply aim to provide a tasty, tactile way for worshipers to connect over coffee and brownies. If an atheist felt the urge to bask in that warm and cozy environment, imagine how potent it must feel to Hillside's believers. Church staff might not be aware, but they are marketing their theology in a sophisticated manner, using an approach that Lindstrom predicts will in future years exemplify how profitable corporations sell their goods around the world.

A variety of people took direct part in Hillside's Sunday service, some making announcements, some comprising a "prayer team," or setting up the communion tables, a few passing the collection baskets. Others performed music.

Two components of the service seemed special, grounded in the here and now. The first was a statement by a wife about her husband who was in the audience. On the podium, Pastor Louie held the microphone for her. She smoothed the skirt of her dress and described her eighty-four year old husband's regimen of dialysis which had ended recently when his kidneys spontaneously revived. The doctors could not explain it; malfunctioning kidneys simply do not renormalize. She said the doctors had used the term "miracle" when releasing him from dialysis. She considered it a miracle and credited the congregation's prayers and good wishes. She said that God had heard their prayers and touched her husband. I recall the congregation responding with a round of applause and the pastor acknowledging the power of prayer and believing. He gave thanks for the husband's recovery.

A bit later there was a "dedication" of an eighteen month old girl. Two parents, two godparents, and one blond toddler named Olivia. Pastor Louie explained that dedications of children follow Biblical teachings to dedicate one's life to God and God's work in the world. Olivia's father spoke first, saying that he'd been raised in the Catholic church. He eventually found Hillside, where he now stood. He wanted his daughter to "feel the community, have the community" that this church offered, along with its spirituality. What he wanted for her was this church family.

When came her turn, Olivia's mother could barely speak through her tears. She said, "Having Olivia changed our lives. Before Olivia, I did not know what unconditional love was." At that earnest statement I had to brush tears from my own eyes. The pastor said a prayer for the family, and asked that the child be touched by Jesus.

Between the music and prayer portions, and the sermon, there was a ten minute break for greeting one another and for the refilling of coffee cups. The buffet was picked clean by the congregation, which was easily one hundred strong. It was during this break that I met a young man named Chris, who with his mother and father shared the table where I sat. Yes, the table. At the perimeter of the worship room were six or seven round tables set with candles that gave off a warm glow in the low lighting. Very soothing, so inclusive and inviting. Joni told me later that the tables were easier for families with small children, and for elders who needed a place to lean against.

I thought then how even teenagers would be hard pressed to resist the coffee, brownies, and easy places to sit, and was reminded of how my mother treated us to ice cream after church on summer Sundays, balancing her requirement for our attendance with the promise of a tasty reward.

My mother had been lonelier in childhood than we four. No siblings, no cousins, her father gone missing during many of her school years (he had left them, remarried, and remained in the same small town, in tantalizingly proximity). She attended one church or another in those years.

I can picture her attraction to a friendly, inviting place where for one day each week she was equal to others, as beloved by God, and comforted by the knowledge that someone heard her prayers. There she could pray for a more attentive mother, for a father to see the error of his ways and return home, for a new dress instead of yet another hand-me-down, for a school janitor who didn't expose himself to students, for a horse, for a brother, and later, for a loving marriage followed by healthy babies to call her own.

Naturally, many prayers are for corrections to problems and ailments already visited on the one praying. I know this because I did my share of praying in my early years, mostly for changes to the status quo. Time, and a flight away from home corrected things for me. I wonder now how many of my mother's childhood prayers were answered. For sure, the one regarding babies.

At Hillside I admired smiling children at their parents' sides and in their parents' arms and recalled attending church with the arbiter of our daily lives. Sunday School was a part of it, as was learning Bible stories and proverbs, and "The Golden Rule." There was even once a church summer school that exuded the smell of Elmer's glue, graham crackers, and those waxy half-pints of milk.

At the break, Pastor Louie reminded parents that children were welcome to remain throughout the entire service provided they were under control, and as long as parents kept them close at-hand for sharing the worship experience. Otherwise, children could adjourn to Sunday school classes down the hall.

I cannot credit worship service as teaching a young child anything beyond conformity and how to function in a church community (and perhaps in Hillside's case to love the smell of sugared air). Kids first learn mimicry. In Sunday school they memorize lessons and make age-appropriate friends or acquaintances. But learning Psalms and aphorisms seems a great remove from actually knowing what religion, or having faith, means on a personal level. Children are simply not capable of assessing the relevance or value of the beliefs being taught. Their aim is to please the person who brings them there, to gain praise, or allay fears, or perhaps to earn an ice cream cone. For the most part, as children we absorb what we are told, accepting that the earth is round when we have no means by which to verify, and that a baby robin grows inside a sky-blue egg until it breaks out into the world.

I listened and memorized and passed the Methodist sniff test for years. I didn't realize then that at that time I was what would be called a skeptic. No one explained the many other choices. I simply knew that the Christian creed held no spark or glow like that which came from mastering algebra, or tinkering with poetry, or understanding the simplest fragment of Spanish. When I think back now I can liken my early thoughts about church and its modes of worship to knowing that there is no Santa Claus but going along with all the preparations and rituals because, well, that is how things worked (the presents, of course, were a nice payoff).

Pastor Louie, who I came to understand is Joni's husband, gave Hillside's homily. He was dressed in jeans and a casual button-front shirt, looking as much like a neighbor or a friend from work as the spiritual leader of a growing community church.

It was the eleventh week in a series of examinations of the Holy Spirit. Louie preached, in part, about how "We don't need another moral person." He said, "We don't need more good people. We need more people who live through God."

He didn't explain that assertion, though perhaps Foursquare followers intrinsically understand. I'll posit an explanation from my novice's perspective. Perhaps Pastor Louie meant that good deeds and good work are insufficient if people don't also know God and believe in God. That such actions as work, moral behavior, and kind words, are not the path to salvation because salvation is gained only through believing the "right way," the evangelical Christian way.

A scholar and lecturer named Robert Oden put it like this: In ancient times there were many Christian factions (including Jewish Christians) holding disparate beliefs as to whether Jesus was the son of God or just a man, which stories about his life were deemed authoritative, and which accounts should be interpreted literally or else symbolically. There were also, over time, opposing factions who debated whether worshipful *behavior* was as important as *believing*. Some felt that beliefs overshadowed an act of worship or other "right behavior," that people needed to believe in Jesus as savior regardless of their own personal and public behavior. Eventually, the faction in favor of belief won out.

I doubt Pastor Louie would say that people's behavior doesn't matter, or that Christians shouldn't also be good or moral. I'd bet that he harbors reasonably high expectations of Foursquare believers, and perhaps all Christians. Because beliefs are a product of thought, and actions follow from thought, then those who think in a Christ-like manner might behave in a Christ-like manner. Even lapsed believers and various skeptics I've spoken with this last year value certain Christian teachings that advocate moral behavior. They would say it's not the believing, but the behavior that matters.

Hillside's communion was self-serve, with congregants choosing wafers and thimbles of juice from tables at the front. Almost everyone participated.

Communion was a part of the Methodist ritual that I liked. I can't say now how often it occurred (surely not every week as in the Catholic Church). Even in my youth I recognized that miniature objects exerted a pull on me. Thus it was that drinking from a doll-sized juice cup was a particularly fine tradeoff for sitting through a Sunday service.

As the Hillside crowd began to break up, I visited a bit more with the young man sharing my table, a musician who had once traveled with his rock band. He had written and recorded a religious song that was at that very moment playing in the background. We discussed storytelling through books and song, and the need for authentic experience to inform our compositions. I invited him to send me an email describing how he came to choose this particular church community, and his views regarding Heaven. Soon thereafter his wife arrived with their young daughter, and he introduced us. The crowd was thinning out and I took my leave.

My notes from that morning reflect that the sanctuary contained no windows. There was a stenciled quote from scripture: Hebrews 13:8, which reads "Jesus Christ

is the same yesterday and today and for ever." Illustrated on the front right wall were the four symbols repre-
senting the Foursquare theology.

On the way to my car I passed by the young musician. He, his parents, and his wife were debating where
the family should have lunch. It's possible he later saw
my website's reference to being an atheist researching
churches, and such insight destroyed any chance I
might have had to ask him further questions. Or he is
simply a busy husband and father, son, employee, and
musician. Our last contact was high on a hill in the
parking lot of a Foursquare church that looks over the
valley below.

4

There Must be Something
to the God Thing

While I didn't get the chance to ask the Hillside musician about Heaven, others have shared their views with me. Janet P is the sixty-something wife of a dentist friend from California, a tennis player who loves the high desert where we sometimes camp during upland game bird hunting season. One afternoon we take a hike along a rambling spring in Nevada's backcountry, poking around abandoned campsites for discarded antique glass bottles and jars. Naturally, I ply her with questions.

Janet attended Methodist, Catholic, Lutheran, and Christian Science churches in her childhood. Her father, a Navy man, was intent upon attending church whenever and wherever the family made its home. She married a disbeliever, though, and he plotted for them a wide berth around organized religion. They saved Sundays for non-church family activities with their sons.

Janet trails me through the tall sage as she describes a trip to Salt Lake City where one of her married sons lives. During the visit, she and her husband went to see the Mormon Tabernacle. Not being members they couldn't go inside, but surrounding it was a grand park-like space with strands of lights strung in the trees. "Just being there. It made you feel ... beautiful. But then I looked around and there were all these *children* pushing children in strollers." She shakes her head. "Really young mothers having children."

Janet believes in a "higher power" because "something must have started all this, the earth and all." When I ask if that entity influences our daily lives, she says, "People have to use their logic to decide that." For her, daily influence by a creator would defy explanation for why some people die young and others do not, and why there are, for instance, terrible cancers. Also, "especially for poor people, and people feeling low," the idea of a higher power "gives people hope. Hope is a good thing." She prays informally, offering up a prayer when it seems needed. In her youth she learned that people shouldn't pray for themselves, only for others.

When I ask if there is a Heaven, Janet says, "probably not." She dislikes Christians who act pious while posturing to solidify their church positions, and who when not in church seem to act unChristian-like. One more thing: There was a man named Jesus, a thinker. He did exist but "he was just a man."

A Paiute-Shoshone woman told me, "There must be something to the God thing because every race on Earth believes in a creator." She herself doesn't believe in Heaven. Even so, she explained the following to me with a wry smile: Whenever one of the family's pets dies, she and the others comfort her young granddaughter with the assurance that the animal has gone to Heaven.

5
Let the Sun Shine In

~~ First Church of Christ, Scientist,
        aka "Christian Science" ~~

his was another Christian denomination I needed for my novel, so I visited the only one listed in our area, which happens to reside in a mixed-use residential neighborhood. The church's members must derive pleasure from its architecture every time they gaze upon its modern, flowing lines and the spire-like projection thrusting up from curved walls.

On a sparkling, late fall Sunday, a gentleman held the door open for a string of ladies entering the airy foyer. With me was Lisa M, a friend of many years. The worship space is smaller than those of other churches I surveyed, but striking in a way I have not experienced at anytime elsewhere. Inside, natural light floods the worship space through a full wall of glass. A few pendant lights hang high overhead, supplementing the room's sunny glow. The inclusion of natural light and a view to trees and desert sky suggest that nature holds equal import to the gently curving wood pews and the simple, elevated podium and lectern.

The service proved entirely different from other Christian services I've known. There were readings of prescribed Bible passages for that particular calendar date, and an organist accompanying traditional Christian hymns. Two mature women led the service. During certain segments the leaders were joined by a young vocalist or another reader. But mostly it was two impeccably-groomed "Readers" directing the flow of the service. And then at the point where there might otherwise have been a sermon, there were more prescribed readings of Bible passages with corresponding interpretations provided by the Mother Church. I later learned that church members elect the Readers who serve during services. No single person, no minister or pastor or priest, is the sole deliverer of the teachings.

As with Foursquare Gospel, the First Church of Christ, Scientist was founded by a woman, in this case Mary Baker Eddy. While it was interesting to note how the Church's interpretations varied from their corresponding Bible passages. The controlled delivery of them almost put me to sleep.

Clearly, that calm would attract followers looking beyond literal interpretations of the Bible, and those eschewing Christian bands belting out gospel rock. No come-as-you-are in jeans and t-shirts or running suits or football jerseys. No coffee break, no turning to greet others sitting nearby, and yet ... it suits people. That one Sunday, silver-haired attendees outnumbered younger ones, but I was told that children attend Sunday school classes which meet during the service.

Though that Christian Science service induced inertia in me, a newbie to its particular tone, I soon discovered that its adherents can embody a lively passion for its tenets. In the church's Reading Room my companion and I found one of its true advocates—Sue Mayes-Smith—who greeted us warmly and encouraged us to browse around. She was meeting with other Sunday

school teachers but took a minute to share a few insights. I cadged a business card from her and we made
an agreement to meet later for a discussion of Christian
Science, which she had embraced after trying various
other denominations.

In the lobby I picked up two free issues of *The Christian Science Monitor*, an award-winning international
news magazine covering subjects such as war, politics,
and humanitarian issues. Only in its last page or two are
there any mentions of religion, any proselytizing. The
publishing arm of the Mother Church also issues a
weekly, *Christian Science Sentinel*, and the *Christian Science Journal*, which contains testimonials from readers.
The textbook they use is *Science and Health*. The
movement's website, www.Spirituality.com, offers weekly lessons, testimony regarding healings, and commentary by individuals who are not necessarily followers of
Christian Science.

On another day I meet Sue for coffee, at which point she
explains that Christian Science sees itself as a movement, not a religion. As such, there are no missionaries
tasked with recruiting new members. Lessons presented
in Sunday services center on a theme drawn from passages found throughout the Bible. The Bible is viewed as
literature, not the literal word of God. Some passages do
not require an interpretation while others are deemed
allegory, for instance, the Book of Revelations. The Bible
is meant to inspire people to find completeness through
individual study.

God is not an entity but a state of being, a state of
love. "God is love," says Sue, meaning God equals love,
and Love therefore is God. And, Jesus was the son of

God, "through his own understanding and oneness [with] God." He was a "seer."

Sue explains that it is human nature to strive for completeness. All people need eventually to realize what they are meant to know and how they are meant to live. Christian Science points the way to enlightenment and fulfillment through seven elements which embody a complete life: Love, Mind, Soul, Principle, Life, Truth, Spirit.

In Sunday school, adults teach young people to apply their own thoughts to problems, to look inward for answers through intellect and self-healing. They work on raising consciousness. In Christian Science, prayer is a private, individual activity. Says Sue, the Lord's Prayer, common to all Christian denominations, is the only prayer spoken aloud and the "Our Father" reference within it refers to any "Father of mankind." Therefore, it includes the creator believed by any person of any religion.

She grants that some Christian Scientists might view traditional western medicine as a last resort, relying first on prayer for healing, since healing works from the inside-out, engaging emotions, spirituality, and conscience in producing a physical outcome. She and her family have experienced just such results, but when doctors diagnosed her father with cancer, he received chemotherapy treatments because he and the family understood that they posed the greatest immediate promise.

I wanted to talk about Heaven and Christian Science's perspective. Sue, who can be viewed as a teacher within the movement, describes Heaven not as a place, but an "understanding of that oneness" with God as

Love. It's a state of mind, "a realization of goodness" and a "human journey." There is no physical journey to Heaven, simply the belief that all *good* expresses the seven elements, and "Heaven is the state of knowing that we are the expression of these things."

In this version of the afterlife, one's state of mind continues as the body turns to dust. It's a crossing over from the physical to pure thought. "We don't lose ourselves as an idea of God," says Sue. On the other side, communication is between God and man, not between people, which means "There *is* an other side. People are still there."

This made me ask about ghosts. Apparitions, she says, are those who have unfinished work, reasons to remain connected to the physical life. What about angels? Angels are "divine messages" from God, God's thoughts passing to man. And, the afterlife is a divine state of mind which will be experienced by *all* people, not just Christian Science believers.

As I transcribed my notes later I realized that Christian Science, more than any other, aligns with beliefs ascribed to the Pueblo Indians of the New World in the National Public Broadcasting Service series titled "God in America." Pueblo spiritual traditions viewed their way of life as good and whole and worthy of reverence, embracing the natural world around them, the fields and mountains, the sun and rain, and all the creatures found therein. They didn't believe in one true God for all the people of the world. This brought the wrath of the Catholic Church, whose enforcers were the Franciscan friars, tasked with conquering and converting the various indigenous peoples of North America. Left to their own beliefs, the Pueblo and other tribes may have nurtured beliefs that looked to the individual for strength and employed non-traditional healing through elements of the natural world plus prayer.

Months after my visit with Sue, I purchased an old reference book and found tucked within its pages a small, one-color flyer listing the tenets of Christian Science. On the front is a seal bearing a cross and crown (registered trademarks of the Trustees under the Will of Mary Baker G. Eddy). The seal's wording reads: *HEAL-THE-SICK-RAISE-THE-DEAD*CLEANSE-THE-LEPERS-CAST-OUT-DEMONS. The copyright shows 1889, 1892, 1894, 1901, 1906, 1908, renewed 1920, 1922, 1934, 1936.

The Tenets read:

As adherents of Truth, we take the inspired Word of the Bible as our sufficient guide to eternal Life.

We acknowledge and adore one supreme and infinite God. We acknowledge His Son, one Christ; the Holy Ghost or divine Comforter; and man in God's image and likeness.

1. We acknowledge God's forgiveness of sin in the destruction of sin and the spiritual understanding that casts out evil as unreal. But the belief in sin is punished so long as the belief lasts.

2. We acknowledge Jesus's atonement as the evidence of divine, efficacious Love, unfolding man's unity with God through Christ Jesus the Way-shower; and we acknowledge that man is saved through Christ, through Truth, Life, and Love as demonstrated by the Galilean Prophet in healing the sick and overcoming sin and death.

3. We acknowledge that the crucifixion of Jesus and his resurrection served to uplift faith to under-

stand eternal Life, even the allness of Soul, Spirit, and the nothingness of matter.

4. And we solemnly promise to watch, and pray for that Mind to be in us which was also in Christ Jesus; to do unto others as we would have them do unto us; and to be merciful, just, and pure.

At the bottom is a facsimile of Mary Baker Eddy's signature.

This small tract seems to contain an early version of tenets that may or may not today be followed by adherents of Christian Science. There are references to a supreme and infinite God, a Holy Ghost, and man in God's image and likeness, while Sue had described God as "not an entity but a state of being, a state of love," and Jesus as the son of God through his oneness with that state of being and love. She and I had not talked about the movement's view of sin or whether man is saved through Christ, through his demonstrations of healing the sick and overcoming sin and death. Had we visited longer those subjects might have come up. I wouldn't be surprised to find that as with literature, the arts, cultural norms, and language, religious tenets evolve and change over time. Christian Science appears no different in that regard.

6

Believers Drive the Business

S ome years back a friend of mine took her young stepchildren to church. It seemed a good thing to expose them to spiritual ways of thinking. The church they attended was particularly inclusive and welcoming, but she found it highly focused on money, always wanting financial commitments from attendees. She didn't have money to commit at the time, didn't feel she could spare any, and that drove her away from the church, which she had meant for the children to experience—an apt example of one challenge facing churches these days.

Churches clearly have a place in America's culture, as symbols of faith, as meeting places for like-minded individuals, as providers of tangibles and intangibles. In spite of any notions about their special status and the spirit by which they function, they operate without the direct patronage of government or royalty. It should then come as no surprise that they must exchange their goods and services for some form of funding.

Churches run on money as do all for-profit and most not-for-profit ventures. They might have mortgages or rent to pay, monthly utilities, they need supplies, and most of them employ some staff (even if part-time): music directors, office help, and building and grounds maintenance. A church's spiritual head is the #1 employee, its chief executive officer. I dare say that person must prove entrepreneurial—organizing, managing, and shouldering the risks of operating an enterprise. Successful entrepreneurship requires creativity and problem-solving skills.

For simplicity's sake, let's call the head-of-church the "preacher." The preacher has a duty not only to serve the church's current patrons, but to build its following. For a church to remain solvent it needs steady revenues; if revenues grow, that is better yet. In our capitalist economy, church followers are customers of the goods and services a church provides. Goods can be tangibles, such as communions, baptisms, weddings, funerals, weekly worship services, Bible study, sickbed visits, and counseling. Intangibles might include homilies that teach life lessons, a feeling of community, spiritual inspiration, and a path to salvation. As the cost of living grows for the surrounding community, so grows the cost of conducting this business of faith. And, the larger the organizational structure, the greater the revenue requirements.

There are at least two avenues by which to fulfill a need for revenue: 1. Increase the price each customer pays (donates); or, 2. Increase the number of participants contributing funds. Since all donations and gifts from participants are entirely voluntary, a church might best attempt to gain more members during a time when fewer have the means to contribute.

I spent almost two decades in the marketing industry working with clients, writers, graphic artists, and media planners. Those years granted me an insider's recognition of the influence of marketing on virtually all public transactions, even some deemed benign, including a few that appear altruistic. Though I don't participate in God-belief, I don't wish ill for churches. I wouldn't promote their failure any more than I'd promote the failure of other legitimate, legal enterprises. They are, however, businesses of a sort. I can't be the only one who sees them in this light.

Today, marketing colors virtually every public transaction. Since churches participate in our culture of exchange, they too use and benefit from marketing. There's the direct appeal: This is where a spokesman asks customers to pay what they can to keep the business running. One assertion might be that Yes, times are tough, but now is not the time to withhold support for God's work. Now is the time to give what you can to keep the church alive, keep alive the church's mission and the Word. This call to action was made by the preacher at Potter's House. In a calm tone he reminded the member-clients gathered there to continue to give to the church even through tough times. Naturally, he was protecting his job and his congregation's physical home. Who wouldn't protect his own slice of the world, especially if he believed that it also provided a conduit to a shared common good and a valuable belief system?

TV and radio broadcasting are forms of marketing we all recognize. They aim to deliver a specific message to a large audience.

Door-to-door "witnessing" is a personal, direct delivery of the message, which might include the sharing of printed materials, Bibles or other religious tracts. Remember when virtually all nightstands in hotels and motels contained a Bible? That's marketing.

Then there's direct mail. While I was writing this book I received a small mailer soliciting subscriptions to *Friends Journal*, a magazine of the Religious Society of Friends, at 55% off the cover price. The appeal, over the signature of Susan Corson-Finnerty, Publisher and Executive Editor, describes the magazine as full of "authentic, Spirit-centered voices" articulating "Quaker values of honesty, integrity, community, simplicity, harmony, and peace." It's an attractive, illustrated piece that shows the Friends Publishing Corporation return address as Philadelphia, PA. I had to wonder how I, an individual who had not requested contact, had been chosen to receive this offer. My educated guess is that FPC employed a direct mail service to align my current literary subscriptions with the reader profile they desire.

The Catholic Church has one or more bloggers helping to spread its theology. Other churches could do the same. Each could have a Facebook community page where its members post prayers for the community and the world, or a *Pinterest* page with photos and affirmations. Members could also post devotional YouTube videos or podcasts. Churches might team up to develop a smart phone application for locating places of worship (handy for travelers, or for locals shopping for a worship home).

Many churches, much like big box retailers, encourage membership. When infants are baptized or "dedicated," they become church members at their parent's behest. Adult members can pledge themselves to a church as well. Hillside's Covenant of Membership reads:

> As a Christ-follower who recognizes that Jesus Christ is the center of my life, I now am led by the

Holy Spirit to join in agreement with my fellow
Christ-followers that the Hillside Foursquare
Church family is where God has placed me to grow
& mature in my relationship with Him & with others ...

~ to find, understand, & follow God's plan for my
  life ...

~ to grow with the vision, purpose, & mission of my
  church family...
  In doing so, I commit myself to God & to my
  church family.

1. I choose to LOVE, OBEY, FOLLOW & GROW in
   Christ in every area of my life
   ~by looking to obey & put into practice
   God's commands
   ~by staying connected to Him, so that I can
   be fruitful & grow in Him
   ~by living as the Monday Morning
   Church, Christ's representative of
   Good News in the world & circle of influence that I have
   John 1:12 - John 15:1-11

2. I choose to believe in, trust, respect, & follow
   my church leaders, & take the direction they
   take ...
   ~by acknowledging that they're placed into
   leadership by God
   ~by praying for them regularly
   ~by following & supporting them into the
   calling & ministry of my church family
   Ephesians 4:11-13 — 2 Thessalonians 3:1,
   2 Hebrews 12:17 — 1 Corinthians 11:1

3. I choose to LOVE, SPEND TIME, & SERVE WITH my church family ...

 ~by actively participating in the life of Hillside

 ~by giving my life to serve others in love

 ~knowing that if I want to grow, I will stay connected to God & to the family

 Galatians 5:13-15 — Philippians 2:12-15 — Hebrews 10:25

4. I choose to believe in my church family enough to stand with it financially ...

 ~by living a faith-filled, disciplined & self-controlled life that God can bless

 ~by giving time, energy, & finances to invest in our church family

 ~by viewing God as my provider, & returning an investment into His Kingdom

 Matthew 6:33 — Malachi 3:10 — 2Corinthians 9:6-12

5. I choose to be a person who is willing to obey God — with all of my heart, soul, mind & strength, & to love others like myself...

 ~by discovering & utilizing with joy my gifts & talents

 ~by taking the time to serve other people

 ~by saying "YES!" to the Holy Spirit instead of "no"

 1Peter 4:10 — Philippians 2:3-7 — Philippians 3:12-14 — Acts 1:8

The back of this folded form has lines for signature and date, and a separate insert reads: "I agree with the Hillside Foursquare Church family Covenant of Membership & affirm my membership in this church family with my signature:" followed by spaces for a signature, mailing address, phone number, and email address.

Membership stands on a higher psychological rung than does simple participation; it infers privilege plus a measure of responsibility. Members *belong.* When they sign on as members they pledge loyalty. The loyalty factor plus a member's cash investment over time will cement a member's patronage, making it harder to change allegiances. Church leaders surely know this and must hope it holds. Hillside is clearly stating its expectations of members, including obedience, loyalty, and financial support. They know that members are more likely than casual visitors to purchase the church's tangible and intangible products.

Churches dealt in the psychology of membership long before retail membership stores were twinkles in the eyes of their founders, thus the practice during centuries past of the "purchasing" of family pews in a show of wealth that elevated a family's status within the church and the community. A friend of mine notes that long ago a Catholic could purchase "indulgences" for his sinful behavior through transactions that were more openly acknowledged as an act of commerce than we admit today.

In October 2010, the Chrystal Cathedral, the huge televangelist church located in southern California known for the program "The Power Hour," filed for bankruptcy. Its home was a steel and glass edifice on the magnitude of European cathedrals, all towers and gleam, a tribute to the magnificence of religion and to those who glorified bigger as better. The Cathedral declared a debt of more than fifty million dollars. I haven't a clue how the business was run, who made money from it, or which creditors got stiffed. There undoubtedly were problems with its business model as well as its member's appetites and abilities to continue purchasing the Cathedral's products during a collapsing economy. All I can say is that $50 million would have bought a boatload of communion wafers.

A USA Today story in April 2011 cited *Outreach Magazine*'s ranking of "The Five Largest U.S. Churches" being two in Texas, one in Georgia, one in Illinois, and one in Kentucky, with attendance ranging from 19,230 to 43,500 per weekend. One of these super-locations is a refurbished sports stadium, proof that the business of big churches remains alive and well.

7
Evangelical Quilts

On a golden October day I sat in my parked car at the look-out on Windy Hill, recalling a bit of good fortune from the previous summer when a couple in my neighborhood held a moving sale before relocating to warmer climes. The wife explained how they could not take everything with them on their move to Henderson, Nevada, where the husband's sister lives.

The treasure I found among their sale items was a half-dozen handmade quilts that the husband's mother had produced starting in the late 1930s. He recounted being six or so and seeing his mother, Ann Cooper, and other church ladies working together on quilts. For the twenty years since Ann's death, the couple had simply stored the quilts, transporting them from one home to the next whenever they moved.

The first one I examined had names stitched onto it as part of the pattern and the story came out that the names were congregants served by Mrs. Cooper's husband, an evangelist preacher. Reverend Onie Cooper started a church wherever the couple lived, and as the couple and their children migrated west from Ohio, he founded churches along the way.

The oldest of the Cooper quilts sports a variety of stitched names along with two dates: November 1939, and January 1940, a time when people would have carried with them their experiences of the Great Depression and the Dust Bowl era. I keep trying to picture some of those church people: Johnnie and Inez, Julia Caldwell, Mrs. R. F. Nicely. In my mind they have dark hair and the quiet smiles of small town folk who know their neighbors and their neighbors' neighbors.

The late 1930s were a time of upheaval in Europe with Hitler's gang on the march and the United States yet to join the fray. I can't help but think that there must have been church families whose sons or husbands eventually left their tiny home town to fight in WWII, leaving loved ones back home praying for their safe return.

I tried to find out more about the church where Reverend Cooper had officiated and whether surviving relatives of the quilters might want to see the quilt or have it for the church. It seemed a fitting example of people's hands at work in concert, and I would have given it back to them. The expression "back" comes to mind because the church community produced that quilt.

After a bit of internet research I called two churches in that Oklahoma community and spoke to a woman who recognized a few of the family names. The church was still there, with its fourth or fifth preacher since those earlier days. The original quilters were long gone, though, and the subsequent generations might yet live around those parts, or not; she didn't know. One woman I spoke with knew the daughter of one of the families, but would not give out an unlisted phone number. The trail of clues wobbled to an end.

Now whenever I run my hand along the blocks of that quilt I picture a handful of women who had survived tougher times than many of us will ever know. With chairs drawn close around a quilting frame they pass the pieced blocks from hand to hand, admiring how the slices of printed flour sacks complement the solid colored fabrics before hand-stitching each to the next. The quilt grows larger by the hour. In running stitches they apply names from family Bibles: Mrs. Baughn, Bernice Smart, John P Hutton, Miss Georgie Dinger, Gussie Ratliff, linked by black thread on clean cotton, and linked through the church where they met and worshiped, where during any given Sunday's service they prayed for those who lay ill at home, and later, for the men who had gone to war.

8

A Hope-shaped Hole

W hen visiting Hillside Church I was given a CD recording of a September 19, 2010 presentation made to an audience gathered at the church. The speaker was James Cook, reverend/ evangelist/ author and a friend of Hillside's pastor and his wife. I can tell from the speaker's voice and certain of his references that he is not a young man. He quotes liberally from the Bible and speaks with a folksy ease.

Maybe if I were a Foursquare follower I'd get some other interpretation (or maybe Cook is not aligned with Foursquare), but I've listened to this Cook recording three times and to me it sounds like he thinks people are mistaken to find transcendence in nature or to see God manifested there.

A few minutes into his presentation he says, "The church is not about meeting. The church isn't about itself at all. The church is not self-focused. The church is the *only* clear representation of Jesus, and therefore of a revelation of the Father that there is in the world, period. God is not revealed through mountains, rivers, sunsets, solitude. You can go contemplate your navel on top of a mountain and think that you feel something, but I'm telling you, that mountain will never reveal God to you. But once he is revealed to you that mountain can have significance. The only way God is revealed is through his body, the church."

I'm not sure whether by "church" the Reverend Cook means little-c church, any gathering of like-minded believers, or capital-C Church, with a hierarchy of leaders and officials. Or maybe he means Cook's church, the specific one he's affiliated with. Either way, it seems that the Reverend is saying that without a church bringing God's word to people there would be no way to know God, that a church must assume leadership in bringing people to God and God to people. Without a church people would not, could not, know God.

I have to wonder, then, how people throughout the world worship God when they have no physical church, only their own beliefs and dreams and hopes. Or if early Christians (or other believers) were wrong to believe in a creator when they didn't belong to a formal group. Before there was the modern Christianity of Reverend Cook, there were early forms of Christianity, some of which included plural gods.

Before those times there were other forms of worship during which people revered yet earlier forms of creators and otherworldly influences. Without contemplating the natural world and its astonishing life forms and machinations, why would people need to contemplate a creator at all? Leave out nature and you negate any need to make order of the world. And why credit God with installing or guiding or perfecting the natural world and its natural beings without first having gazed upon a mountain or a sunset and therein detected something grander than just craggy peaks or pink and purpling rays?

My sense is that the Reverend is preaching that the hierarchy of a church, the structure and leadership and the church's interpretation of gospel is the only path to belief. That even contemplative individuals cannot know God without association through a church. Are we to think then, that early believers without churches were ignorant about God? Were they not some of those whose beliefs led to the modern Christian church that Reverend Cook benefits from? He seems to be saying that it's not about a private and personal examination of how and why the world works, or an individual's need to believe in a creator. Church provides the only path to God; start with church, he says.

I, for one, feel most connected to all living things while gazing at an ocean vaster than my eyes can behold, while hiking through a stand of Jeffrey pines, or admiring fat bunches of arrow-leaf balsamroot among the rolling foothills of the Truckee Meadows.

In the wide open under a turquoise sky I feel both small and large, smaller than the peaks and valleys, than the steep-sided canyons and sure-footed bighorn, and large enough to appreciate the dependence of all creatures upon the natural elements, and each other.

The breeze brushing past me at those moments has conceivably touched all other forms: clouds, water, people. It circles the planet, nourishing all. I am not persuaded by Cook's narrow view. He can dismiss nature as inconsequential without altering my perspective one whit.

That said, I do like the opening statements of Reverend Cook's presentation which include reminders to "value this moment," that once this moment passes it will never be repeated. Here's Cook: "This moment is the only one there is, and then it's gone, just a recent memory."

Then he says that this life is not about what each future moment holds, but about living well right now, today. Words that sound humanistic, even a bit Buddhist, in touch with an appreciation of the here and now as opposed to what may or may not come after this life, come to think of it, slightly resembling what little I know about Christian Science and its emphasis on seeking a path to personal peace, to wholeness and love in each moment and hour. Christians, in spite of their church's dogma, must also contain humanist leanings, in that humanists seek to encourage others toward fulfillment regardless of whether that fulfillment includes organized religion.

I listen to the Cook CD while parked at one of my favorite vantage points in all of Reno. On this fall day, storm clouds gather to advance east toward the tawny foothills and peaks of the Virginia Range. Yellow blooms of rabbit brush herb the air. The city spread out below was built by people, as were the bridges and freeways, the hotel towers and gaudy casinos, the water park, schools, and houses.

I credit those builders for their vision and their sweat equity, but for sometimes wrecking things too. They make love and marry, walk their dogs and sell cars, vote and make music, and write down the stories. Some would say that God's hand is in all these things, that he acts through all people. If we grant the proposition that credits God for even the least of these, then he also must be credited for the murderers and rapists among us and for those who wreck our valley's natural beauty. If there is only one unerring, all-powerful God, his hand must also paint the shadows too, either directly or through an evil agent of his making. Frankly, the notion of Satan seems a patch-kit for the flawed proposition of an inerrant God.

Some will argue that God granted free will to humans, that after making the world he left us to our own devices. Sink or swim. In that context he does not steer each believer, coax each blade of grass to grow, or battle forces of evil. But if God is not directing people's days, why bother to pray? Why ask for intercession to mediate troubles, calm fears, or alleviate sorrow? Why hope for miracles? If a believer cannot expect a sign or an answer from an omnipotent being, one who listens to all and knows all, why should she plead her case?

I know that some scholars and theologians argue that the Bible and God and God's role are too complex to simplify as I do here, too complex to reduce to logic and rational thought. They insist we accept religious teachings and lesson on *faith* because the nature of faith is that it contains mystery and miracles. It pulses with the unanswerable. In my brain that proposition acknowledges and invites illogical, irrational thought to rise up, suspended in thin air over the empty footprints where logic and pragmatism could otherwise walk.

I would argue that it's *people* who are too complex to dismiss in favor of faith. The workings of our physical bodies, our brains and emotions, are sometimes confounding, enough so that science and medicine unravel their mysteries at a glacial pace. The enigmatic beauty of humanity is in its infinite variety and knotty intricacies. When we dismiss a human being's extraordinary characteristics in favor of ascribing an outside unseen force we risk devaluing the compelling, if messy, grandeur we each contain. I marvel at the wondrousness within us but I don't look elsewhere to credit the fabulous conundrum that is a human being.

It seems to me that believing in God or Yahweh or Allah, or any deity, grows out of people not believing sufficiently in humanity, in themselves, in their own resilience and capacity to grow and to find sufficient nuggets of satisfaction embedded in an average day. When cultural or economic forces sprout dark shapes and fail to meet people's needs, or when safety and control are at risk, when this life, this day, this moment is not enough, people look beyond themselves for something more. But when we ascribe the world's workings to God and his will, we deny our own complicity in its successes and failures. How easy it is to leave credits and faults in someone else's hands. While we're at it, we might as well blame the dog for our homework gone missing.

I grant that I speak from a relatively privileged position, with a roof over my head and the means to buy groceries, certainly the basics and some of the extras. I'm not addicted to drugs or alcohol, sex or shopping, not belittled or beaten by my husband. I don't have disabled children needing 24-hour care. I don't live under a repressive regime or a dictatorial autocrat. Literature and the arts are not censored here. I don't pay taxes to maintain self-appointed royalty, nor in my town do armed militias run the midnight streets bent on rape and dismemberment at the point of a machete. I'm not rich, but I am not poor or downtrodden.

I feel lucky indeed for all of the above, but unlike many others in this same relative comfort I don't think there ought to be some golden reward for walking a reasonably moral path and not damaging too many people along the way. Curiosity rises up in me when I imagine people subscribing to a future that is sweeter than the everyday they now experience. The need, the desire for an easier, more golden afterlife makes the most sense for people who are oppressed, marginalized, unfairly imprisoned, or enslaved. And for those conscripted to murder others, or abused and neglected without reprieve—people living under not just the weight of poverty but under duress from debasing circumstances they cannot change. Under those circumstances I understand the need to hope for something more civilized and more fulfilling. Under those circumstances I would hunger for a better future too.

In January I attended a large west coast writers' conference which included, as most do, luncheons where writers can network with others writing the same genre (self-help, romance, suspense, non-fiction, etc.). The gentleman next to me described his research on the subject of religious extremists abroad and in the U.S. Within that context he used the term "God-shaped hole" to represent the despair felt by people who fill their empty places with a religious extremism which condones murder in the name of God/ Yahweh/ Allah. He also mentioned his own background as Catholic; he'd been an altar boy. No wonder he used the term God-shaped hole for what to me seemed a description of a Hope-shaped hole, a void in emotional fulfillment that needs filling.

For many people around the globe there is no reason to expect that life might grow gentler and more humane. Sadly, it may never become more satisfying or enlightened. For them then, hope might only arise in the promise of a heavenly afterlife earned through heeding admonitions to Walk this way, Do as I say, All points lead to the promised land.

For many of the rest of us, though, I wonder what is so awful or scary about owning our lives, for good and ill? Why not stand accountable to each other and all who populate this planet, and to the earth itself? No promises of some future glory, a cherished place of honor, a passel of virgins. No being someone different over there or up there—better, happier, less competitive, at peace. Why is it not enough to be simply ourselves, glorious and fallible, grateful and glad?

Isn't it enough that the full moon
washes the deck's potted flowers with
an artist's palette of pale blues and starlight?
Or that creeper vines plying the back fence
glow like flames atop the ivy's resolute green?
Or that honey bees have switched allegiance
from summer's last blooms to
vie with hummingbirds for a cheap drink
of sugared water?
That slim cylinders of metal dangling from
strings turn breezes into unchained melodies,
and water vapor in the sky
forms shapes as singular as snowflakes.
That my husband, after all these years, still
electrifies my mind, my lips, my heart.
That snippets of song rise like smoke
from unseen fires in the space between my ears.
And then there's Petie's pointer-coat
with spots aplenty for new constellations,
if we take a moment to string them together.
We will name them after friends and agree

that such inspired designs
are enough to cause us awe and wonder
without crediting the intervention of Heaven
(wherever that might be,
and whoever might be in charge).

Another thought: Humans, in all their messy glory, are a mere fraction of the occupants of this complex world. A biologist at Canada's Dalhousie University notes that Earth holds almost nine million species and we've only discovered a quarter of them. Said the study's author, Boris Worm (I swear, that's his name), "We are really fairly ignorant of the complexity and colorfulness of this amazing planet." Still, people gaze outward and upward for inspiration.

A family friend of ours married a devout Catholic man, the perfect match, as both are Christian to the core. I've never seen anyone so certain she was blessed. Their firstborn, a daughter, was about three years old when their son was christened. I remember the dark-haired cherub curtseying and genuflecting at the back of their small-town church, and the mother's delight at how her little one made such gestures of respect, how cute she looked while mimicking the adults.

Ten years later, that daughter is a young teen beauty, artistic, and bright. The son has his mother's smile and his father's dashing charm. I picture the family attending church every Sunday, except when the mother's metastatic cancer renders her too ill. Then, perhaps, they pray together and study the Bible at home.

I've heard the saying about God not tasking a believer with more than she can handle, but what if this challenge proves too much? If that's God's will, it's not my idea of goodness, or mercy, or a fair shake for that family. If God received credit for this woman's earlier remission, does he get credit for this newly invigorated foe? And if chemotherapy helped ten years ago, but now the situation is in want of a miracle, did prayers for successful treatment go unanswered that first time around? Perhaps certain prayers are unworthy, or God only answers a percentage, but not necessarily those of the faithful. In that case, why bother to pray?

In *Unbroken*, Laura Hillenbrand's biography of WWII bombardier Louis Zamperini, a plane carrying Zamperini is shot down over the Pacific. He and some crew survive a months-long drift at sea in a raft that is immoderately stocked. After much suffering through physical and mental deprivations, Zamperini bargains with God to survive the ordeal. *If only*.

Eventually the raft drifts a thousand miles and survive he does! But barely, and only to be taken prisoner and subjected to psychological and physical torture and further deprivations. He survives these too, and at war's end returns home to the United States.

But why *him*, of the hundreds of pilots whose planes fell into the sea, why, against seemingly insurmountable odds, did *Zamperini* survive? Did prayer help? I see the answer in how the biographer paints him: as honorable, determined, resourceful, and brave. It seems clear to me that the man helped himself.

You are wondering, perhaps, if I pray for our friend and her family. Well, yes I do. It's just that my type of praying doesn't involve a god. Instead, I entreat innovative research scientists and oncologists to develop yet more viable targeted drugs or else a flat-out cure. Sometimes I lie in bed thinking about this friend and our single conversation about the distance between her beliefs and mine. She took the news of my disbelief with equanimity, saying she would have taken me for a believer; I seem so caring.

Surely, though, she knows other atheists, even if they are hard to tease out from the tangle that comprises a life. My admission may have seemed a shock, yet atheists are as likely to be upstanding, caring, moral citizens as are believers. And on the flip side, as likely to be criminal. Or, wait—if there are more believers than disbelievers, which recent national surveys report is the case, there must by sheer numbers be more believers who are swindlers, rapists, thieves, and murderers. I don't know quite what to make of such statistics, except that perhaps God-belief rivals prison sentences and the death penalty for ineffectiveness as a deterrent to crime.

My worldview probably chafes against this friend's beliefs, and her husband's. Their children have been taught and accept that someday they will again see their deceased great-grandparents and other long-gone relatives. What if the children begin to talk about how people reunite in Heaven? What if, *what if* the subject comes up and I open my big mouth and share my perspective, even in the gentlest way? If such honesty unduly worries these parents, they fail to grasp how a disbeliever can respect their faith and the comfort it brings their family.

9
God-words and Vanilla Curses

My mother prays. She prays every night before she drifts off to sleep, and probably each freezing winter day while attempting to start a car which has not been driven for a week or two. She prayed and worried over a tumor on her side that she'd avoided doctoring for ten years or so. The tumor didn't go away until the surgeon removed it, so I'm not sure what use were all those particular prayers, except that the growth was deemed benign. She told me she had thanked God for that.

She prays me all the way to her house and all the way home again when I drive from Nevada through two states to see her. That's at least two days each way, and she starts in advance too, during the preparatory stages, maybe even back at the beginning point when we first discuss whether I should come for a visit in May or June. I have told her she doesn't need to do all that because I figure she works herself up over enough other worries about any number of life's deficiencies that she doesn't need to spend prayer time on my travel arrangements. But she has convinced me that she has no choice. She needs to pray, plain and simple. Needs to. So she does what she needs to do and I practice safety on the road, along with what I like to think are exceptional driving skills developed over forty years of getting from one place to the next. She thanks God when I pull onto her gravel driveway, and then later when I call to say I'm home again. At that point she cries with joy that I've made it and never quite credits me for getting myself home unscathed, but hey, I'm used to it. That's my mother.

In these, her later years, she has taken to using what I would call vanilla cursing. I'm fairly certain she doesn't mean to blaspheme, but you'll have to take my word for it: they *sound* like curses. When she's particularly miffed about my not obeying her instructions to the letter (you would think that after five decades I would have an adequate grip on techniques of obedience), she will say, "God *help* me."

It's not a prayer. I know this because it's said with irritation while she's stomping into the kitchen and away from further discussion with a willful child who doesn't snap-to. I recognize that it's the same phrasing as a prayer, similar to words being used during the Christian television broadcasts she likes to watch, though perhaps they use more complete sentences, as in a plea for mercy or heavenly intervention. My mother, though, has come to use such phrases as an exclamation, sometimes along with others such as "Dear God." It's the context that gives them the flavor of curses.

Funny thing is, our family didn't swear during our growing-up years. No Jesus, damn, shit, Christ. No shut-up. No body parts like asshole, balls, or dick. No references to farting, shitting, fucking. We adhered to the same standards as the national network broadcasters of the 1960s, eschewing all those words that comedian George Carlin so loved to cut up about. But in the late

1980s when my mother's father suffered a stroke that eliminated most of his verbal skills, one of the words he could speak clearest was "shit," delivered with what I came to admire as a certain monosyllabic eloquence. That word became an all-encompassing, regular utterance, and so my mother grew to tolerate his use of it. What could she do but cut an old man some slack?

God-words have become part of modernity's vocabulary, even mine. In previous decades they might have held weight when sworn aloud. Now they're as common as grass. Credit for their devaluation might be due to how this country has over the centuries institutionalized God-references, inserting them into patriotic songs, oaths and pledges. Anyone with a coin in his pocket, or a dollar bill, carries God-words around, handles them, folds them, passes them along without much thought. Our currency, symbol of capitalist (principally secular) exchanges reads like a marketing tool for God-belief— God-references with each cash purchase of Starbucks, stockings, or sex. My Whirlpool buyer protection policy contains an exemption for "Acts of God," as if God's stamp will be on the next earthquake or tornado that hits Reno.

As I finish this paragraph it is two weeks to Christmas. OMG! Almost everywhere I venture I encounter secular holiday songs mixed up with religious songs and hymns, secular decorations alongside the religious, and a *Merry Christmas* greeting followed by *Happy Holidays!* Christmas doesn't seem all that religious anymore, having morphed into a celebration dominated by materialism and market forces (likewise for Easter). In a bit of quid pro quo, the secular world has appropriated religious celebrations and the Christian world has put its mark on secular instruments and ceremonies. No wonder so many of us use God-words with abandon. Believers might attribute some fleeting import to such words as they exclaim, "Jesus Christ!" but I'd bet not much. The illogical encroachment of God-words into secular life has bleached the starch out of what would have otherwise been solemn invocations of a sacred name. Instead, God-words have settled into the silt of the cliché heap. Credit believers for that.

In the last few years, my mother has on occasion used Grandfather's *shit* word, to good effect. She also practices that tame version of cursing I described. The latter I attribute in part to the God-ubiquity of our culture, which I suppose I ought to object to on non-religious grounds. In truth, I applaud an expanding vocabulary as a good and useful thing.

10
A Cup of Tea and a Spoonful of Heaven

~~Calvary Chapel, Reno ~~

I arranged to meet my husband's cousin and her spouse at their church, which practices a "born-again" Christian theology. As I understand it, to be born-again means that a person already born in the flesh is a second time born in the spirit by accepting Jesus Christ as Lord and Savior.

We met in the church's café, a large and airy space flanked by a wall of north-facing windows. Lettered on the café's wall: "And they devoted themselves to the apostles' teaching and fellowship, to the breaking of bread and the prayers—Acts 2:42." Approximately two dozen other people were enjoying coffee and muffins, sitting for a moment in quiet or making morning talk before adjourning to the sanctuary.

Calvary's sanctuary is similar to that of Potter's House, and of Hillside, with soothing colors throughout and no windows. Modern gospel music filled the room with melody; lyrics flashed on the large screens at the front. The congregation sang three or four songs, which were followed by the pastor's welcoming remarks, and the passing of collection plates along each aisle. The song accompanying the collection included the lyrics, "Oh Lord, we make our offering."

Calvary's senior pastor, Tom Luitwieler, conducted much of the service and gave a sermon which included a prayer for the Church in America. One thing he said was, "The message of the gospel is what our country needs to hear." He meant before it is too late. This put me in mind of a recent network news report on declining church attendance nationwide and a defection of members from traditional organized religion, particularly among younger generations.

Other portions of the service included a review of upcoming local elections as outlined in a handout from the 2010 Christian Coalition titled "Voter Guide." The contests included the U.S. Senate race of Reid v. Angle, Nevada's race for Governor, and a District 3 race. Following those announcements were a number of biblical passages illuminating a topic being examined as part of a weekly series, in this case the "conduct of the Church," which included expectations of the church as a house of God and a spiritual household of its members. The pastor reminded congregants that the conduct of church members reflects on the household (the church).

Communion was taken by virtually all of the people present; I may have been the only one to abstain. In a process novel to my experience everyone kept their seats as baskets of crackers and trays of tiny cups of juice were distributed through the aisles. These "symbols" were then consumed, three hundred hands lifted in concert to three hundred mouths in what struck me as an apt example of a communal communion.

In this church the Bible is the word of God, and the Jews viewed as God's chosen people, which explained the Israeli flag alongside the American flag at the front of the chapel. At Calvary there is no membership application as there was at Hillside Foursquare, but I did see various handouts and lists for signing up for groups and classes. The Weekly Schedule was packed with activities, including "Street Witnessing" and "Street Witnessing Prayer." Its announcements included projects to provide Thanksgiving baskets to families in need, and "Operation Christmas Child," part of a national effort to send hygiene basics and small treats to needy children in other countries. "Ministries Available at Calvary Chapel" listed twenty-six choices. There was a calendar handout for Men's Ministry, and a Prayer Calendar that included prayers for: the Men and Women in our Armed Forces, Gospel for Asia Ministry, Hope for Today/David Hocking, the various pastors and their families, CSN and Radio Ministries, Marriages and Couples, the Peace of Jerusalem, for those out of work, Widows, Home Fellowships, the Persecuted Church, Sunday School Teachers, and more. Clearly, a busy church with a lot of work to do.

After the service I drove toward home as a stout wind shoved leaves along the streets and rain pelted the valley, just enough to require windshield wipers. As I headed west toward downtown the sky brightened a bit as a huge rainbow appeared, its span arcing from the city's western edge to the northern-most foothills (approximately where Hillside Foursquare Church sits). I marveled at it as I drove; it seemed anchored to that upslope of city. At the same time, on the car radio there came a commercial for a Miracle Fair being held at the Reno-Sparks Convention Center. "Need a miracle?" the announcer asked. The voice went on to describe a "mystical, psychic" event which offered miracles.

Suffice it to say that rain seldom falls in the high desert, making rainbows a rare gift. I hurried home to grab my camera and headed south. From atop what is known locally as Windy Hill, where the wind gusted to 60 mph or so that day, I watched the apparition drift toward me. The hilltop to my left obscured one end, but dead ahead two-thirds of it glowed in concentric rings of glorious color. Farther east appeared a fainter, grayer twin.

I steadied my umbrella to shield the camera lens and snapped away until my nylon cover turned itself inside out, forcing me back to the shelter of my car. The banded arc eventually halted within a half-mile from my hilltop lookout. It seemed to hover there.

The rain grew steadier as the clouds overhead thickened. As I started down the hill the colors overhead began to disperse, turning to vapor above the neighborhoods. For a while there, the storm had delivered a bit of the heavens to earthbound watchers such as me.

The day arrives for me to meet cousin Joan at a local coffee shop for a discussion about her religious beliefs. I say "discussion" even though I ask most of the questions and Joanie does most of the sharing. We each order tea, and as I cannot go into one of those places without sampling their baked goods, I choose a chocolate chip cookie. Tea, cookie, good conversation. What more could I ask?

Joan comes prepared to answer my questions, even bringing a printed page of Bible verses pertaining to Heaven. She explains how she found her faith through a need for release from years of guilt and shame that her family and cultural circumstances had heaped upon her. She examined disbelief in various forms, including atheism. She partied and ran around. Her first marriage was unhappy, followed by divorce.

She says, "I got down on my knees and prayed for help. I said, 'I just can't do this anymore', and I asked God for help." A great weight lifted from her once she took Jesus Christ as her savior.

The printout she brings me lists the following passages: John 14:1-4, in which Jesus says, "Do not let your hearts be troubled. Trust in God, trust also in me. In my Father's house are many mansions. If it were not so, I would have told you. I am going there to prepare a place for you. And if I go and prepare a place for you, I will come back and take you to be with me, that you also may be where I am." The next one is Romans 8:38-39, then Revelation 21:1-4. Her notes also indicate a description of Heaven found in the Bible's book of Revelation, chapter 21, verses 11-29:

> It shone with the glory of God, and its brilliance was like that of a very precious jewel, like a jasper, clear as crystal. It had a great high wall with twelve gates and with twelve angels at the gates. On the gates were written the names of the twelve tribes of Israel. There were three gates on the east, three on the north, three on the south, and three on the west. The wall of the city had twelve foundations, and on them were the names of the twelve apostles of the Lamb ... the wall of the city was made of jasper, the city of pure gold. The foundations of the city walls were decorated with every kind of precious stone—jasper, sapphire, emerald, carnelian, topaz ... The twelve gates were twelve pearls ... The city does not need the sun or the moon to shine on it, for the glory of God gives it light, and the Lamb

is its lamp ... Nothing impure will ever enter it, nor will anyone who does what is shameful or deceitful, but only those whose names are written in the Lamb's book of life.

Time flies when I'm talking with a passionate person. Joan describes the most difficult parts of her life, the sharing itself a gift for which I am truly grateful. We talk about Heaven, not only the Biblical promises of its beauty and how one gets there, but what she imagines Heaven might look like, how it might resemble or differ from the Bible's descriptions. For one thing, she loves animals. She says, "I know that my pets are going to be there. In Genesis, God commands man to take care of the animals. He loves his creation; it says so all through the Bible. So, I believe he has a special place for them." She states that animals have suffered broadly on this planet, and God will have taken notice. "I believe he will make it right." In Joanie's Heaven, not only will her mother and other beloved family and friends be present, but her pets, and somewhere too, the wild animals.

An hour and a half passes. Before we part she says, "You know, I try not to be condescending about this, I try really hard not to sound that way, but Dusty and I talk about it sometimes when we think about what the future holds. And I just want to say that I'm going to miss us not being together [with you] for eternity."

We hug. Warmed by her compliment I drive away. Someday I'll be missing her too.

11

Heaven for Hookers

I have given you a feel for the beliefs of some people in my personal sphere, which includes plenty of believers because a person cannot live in America without knowing believers. They're everywhere, and it turns out that some of them reside in a place most readers will not have visited: the world-famous Mustang Ranch brothel east of Reno, just across the next county's line.

I first set foot in Mustang two years ago when researching my first novel, "Morning Without Ruth." A writer friend and I took a tour there—yes, they offer public tours—and at that time met a young hooker who went by the name Daisy. Besides showing us around the main Ranch and what was once Joe Conforte's private apartment, she told us a little about her own background as a rural Nevada girl and how she had found herself in that kind of work. She truly seemed a sweet young thing, with a good presence and a friendly, professional manner.

I felt a fondness for Daisy and I was curious to see if a year later she still worked there. I hoped she might be willing to once more indulge a writer's questions, this time about religious beliefs and Heaven. I suppose I wanted also to learn whether she was doing okay, or perhaps, romantic that I am, that she had indeed saved enough money to make the leap to attending university. As it turned out she was no longer employed there, but I was prepared to query any of the girls who would oblige questions from a stranger.

I drove east on a Monday's noon-hour, hoping to arrive during a lull in the pace of the brothel/ bar/ lounge. Stepping through Mustang's front door is like regressing to a 1970s discotheque. It seems a dark hole if you enter from the bright of day. Then your eyes adjust and details become obvious: flat panel TV screens on the walls showing naked women in sensuous slow-motion; an elevated stage in one corner with a pole for that type of performance; a dozen round cocktail tables with heavy-bottomed swivel chairs; a bar at the far end; and loud music playing in the background. The place reeks of cigarette smoke even when no one is actively lighting up.

Of the five or six girls seated at tables, two give me quizzical looks that telegraph, *Check her out. Could be my mom.* My interview subjects. I step closer and explain my agenda. They agree to visit while consuming the lunches they had chosen from the 4-star menu.

Dark-haired Ashtyn is a two-month veteran of Mustang who arrived with a five-year plan she hoped to complete in three years. She's there for the money, plans to save enough to buy a gas station/mini-mart and also a real estate office, imagining good profit potential for each. She's from the Midwest, raised by Lutheran grandparents, but her grandfather refused the family's attendance at church "because [the church] always wanted money." Instead he led the family in Bible studies at home.

Ashtyn reads the Bible and prays every day. When I ask how she reconciles working as a prostitute with the Bible's teachings, she notes that the people in the Bible "were not all perfect." Point made. And what, I ask, does she pray about? She says, "I pray for forgiveness every day." She believes in Heaven, but "I'm not sure Heaven is going to be beautiful ... This could be Heaven on Earth." She also believes in reincarnation, saying, "I believe I'm an old soul." She makes me wonder if her experiences as a sex worker contribute to her feeling older than her years.

Shawna, also dark-haired, has been at Mustang less than a month, having previously been an independent sex worker. She despises organized religion. "The Bible," she says, "is written by men, so how could it represent God?" She came to this thinking by watching others around her, particularly the so-called Christian parents of a previous boyfriend who refused her a chance to visit him while he lay dying in the hospital. "A lot of religion," she says, "just rubs me wrong." When I ask her about Heaven she said, "I don't believe in anything. When I die, I'm just gone."

Both of these young women view Mustang as a safer workplace than their previous arrangements. Ashtyn, who suffers from social anxieties, freelanced too, until she encountered a man with a knife. At that point she decided to take this newer course. She has a seven-year-old daughter who lives with relatives in the Midwest. When I ask if she sees her daughter on visits home, she blinks and says she hasn't yet, but she will eventually. She plans to.

Mustang Ranch is tucked against steep desert hills that line the Truckee River canyon as it runs east from

Reno. No surprise then that among the crags and hills, radio reception stinks, and it's ironic that the one frequency to come in loud and clear is a Christian station.

It happened that the radio was playing on one occasion when Shawna took a customer to her room. But the man couldn't perform and claimed the music was to blame. What did she do about it? She shrugs as she says, "Just turned the volume down."

A busty platinum blonde joins our conversation. She won't give a name but says she is spiritual, believing in the metaphysical. She explains that every person has energy and that life is an exchange of energy flowing to and from us. Some of her beliefs stem from conversations with a Buddhist hooker who keeps a Buddhist shrine complete with candles and statuary. The girls point her out, a petite Asian wearing red sequins.

The unnamed worker shares one more thought before taking her leave. She says, "When a man puts his seed in you, he's giving you some of his energy." I ask how that works given that Mustang requires the use of condoms during sex. She gives me a blank look, then stands and walks away with her empty lunch container.

Per Ashtyn, spirituality is a regular topic around there. "We talk about it all the time."

My mouth hangs open a moment before I think to snap it shut. Then I say, "Really?"

She nods. "Really. It's what we do when we're in the back. We sit around and talk about all that stuff."

That is the moment when I wish for a hall pass for hanging out with the working girls so I can overhear the conversations they have when they get to let their guard down and pick at their cuticles and imagine a different life, or a different place for the same kind of life, or whatever it is that comes next after this one. I might just do that someday—ask to sit in on a lunchroom discussion. If I ever make that happen, I'll let you know.

When I wrap up my questioning, Ashtyn and Shawna stand, adjust their strapless mini-dresses, and collect their empty Styrofoam containers. With farewell smiles they exit through a doorway leading to a hall.

For my first novel I constructed a fictional brothel set in rural Nevada, complete with a kitchen where most of the exchanges between the working girls take place. I wrote plenty of dialogue between hookers, but I did not include, nor had I imagined, the conversations that Ashtyn and Shawna describe as taking place daily. In their free time, at meals, or when they're off duty, they talk about religion and the afterlife. It's all very respectful. Though they each hold a different view toward faith and religion, atheism, and agnosticism, they also seem to draw inspiration from proximity to the diverse belief systems they discuss.

Here I had thought that working girls would spend their spare time talking about sex, or shopping, or vacations, or family. I guess those subjects must come up too, they'd have to, but for these girls such mundane topics are less a constant than more spiritual matters. It turns out that their personal talk is most often about faith, God, and how they believe or don't, and particularly those matters relating to the hereafter. Perhaps that is because as Ashtyn said at one point, "Almost everyone here has been hurt somehow." When she spoke those words it seemed to me that she wasn't only referring to meeting men who carry knives.

12
To the Temple

~~Temple Sinai–Reform~~
     A Jewish Worship Service

This experience is the toughest one to describe, in part because portions of the service were spoken in Hebrew, but also because of the music and song. There were texts providing transliterations and others guiding the flow of worship, and I tried to follow along. I own no share of the Jewish conscience, the traditions, or language, but from a lecture by Robert Oden, professor and religious scholar, I learned that Judaism focuses on community because Jews as a tribe—not as individuals—were chosen by God.

In a good bit of fortune I picked a September Friday evening during High Holy Days to attend service at the temple, which openly welcomes Jews from other congregations and visitors of all faiths. It was Kol Nidre, an "Aramaic declaration that nullifies all the vows and promises that each person will make to God and to him/herself in the coming year, an acknowledgement of the weakness of human resolution."

Kol Nidre is the eve of Yom Kippur, which means Day of Atonement, the conclusion of a ten-day period of soul searching that begins with Rosh Hashanah, when according to Jewish tradition the names of the living righteous are inscribed in The Book of Life, thereby guaranteeing another year of life. According to a handout providing answers to frequently asked questions, "Yom Kippur atones only for sins between humanity and God, not for sins against another person. To atone for sins against another person, you must first apologize," setting right the wrongs committed, if possible. Tradition states that this righting of wrongs must be accomplished before the end of Holy Days. "Sins in Judaism are not acts for which a person will be punished in the afterlife, but an improper act for which one can ask forgiveness, not only from God, but from human beings as well."

Glass doors led into the worship space. Gentlemen greeted the parishioners streaming in. Eventually, a few hundred people had gathered. Then came rabbi Teri Appleby, with an open, friendly demeanor and a petite, graceful presence.

The service started with an opening prayer set to a haunting soundtrack played by four musicians. When the violin, viola, cello, and piano struck up, here is what happened: My imagination dissolved the nondescript room. It fell away to reveal an ancient city of adobe walls rising up along narrow, sloping lanes leading the faithful to the city's temples and mosques. The music swirled, ushering, calling, lamenting, warning, the sound of tears in the air, the sound of longing. Even I was in that old place, dumb but awed.

The Yom Kippur theme—atonement—is somber, but Rabbi Appleby also spoke about communication, about keeping channels open between family members and spouses, and between co-workers and neighbors. Her message was that we should not lose our human connections in this era of increasing technology and sound bites—a modern message delivered during a traditional service steeped in ritual.

I had requested handouts and texts from the greeters, which I tried to follow as best I could. The service used *The New Union Prayer Book ~ For the Days of Awe.* One prayer read aloud came from page 248:

Once more Atonement Day has come.

All pretense gone,

naked heart revealed to the hiding self,

we stand on holy ground,

between the day that was,

and the one that must be.

In the handouts, the word God is not written out, but represented by "G-d." The pamphlet for the week ahead listed Saturday's Yom Kippur service(s), Talmud study, and Hebrew School classes. Also a meeting of Sisterhood Mahjong Night and an International Folk Dance Night.

Christian worship services typically include music that is either upbeat with simple, catchy lyrics or else drawn from a canon of classical hymns. The latter I recognize from my youth. During this service the voice of cantorial soloist Jonathon Leo was deep and rich. I could not follow the lyrics, but no matter. Yearning and joy translate without words.

On a separate note, the "Faith Forum" column in our local newspaper quoted a reply given by Elizabeth W. Beyer, rabbi of Temple Beth Or, to the question of whether believers should try to convince others to see the "right path" they follow. I like Rabbi Beyer's answer:

Religious diversity has been an accepted norm for Judaism. In Biblical times, non-Jews (ger toshav) also lived in Israel. Torah says, 'you shall love him as yourself' (Lev. 19:34). In the 1100s, the great theologian Maimonides said Christianity and Islam serve to spread knowledge of G-d. Modern Jewish thought agrees.

The path to G-d can be found through a variety of religious choices. Indeed, diverse religions may be necessary in this world and part of the Divine Plan.

There is no requirement to convert people to Judaism in this world or the next.

A majority of people believe that religions other than their own can lead to eternal life (Pew Forum survey on Religion & Public Life). Ancient sages echo that, saying, 'Righteous people of all nations have a share in the world to come' (Sanhedrin 105a, Tosefta). All people have access to G-d and the world to come.

Calvary Chapel, which I visited earlier, displays an Israeli flag, symbol of fundamental Christians' theological support of Jews as God's chosen ones. I now wonder how many of Calvary's congregants have experienced a Jewish worship service. A hundred? Ten? None?

13
Isn't it Worth the Effort?

An article I read in late April 2011 cited a *NEWSWEEK* project challenging a thousand Americans—not immigrants, but American citizens—to take the current U.S. Citizenship test. Fully 29% couldn't name the current Vice President and 73% couldn't attribute the cause of our past involvement in the Cold War. Six out of ten respondents couldn't circle Independence Day on the calendar. The article went on to explain that civic ignorance is nothing new. We're particularly good at it. According to a study by the dean of the Annenberg School for Communication, Americans' civic knowledge has been measured in yearly shifts that average "slightly under 1 percent." That's not saying much about Joe Citizen when born-here types know less about the U.S. than do immigrants who diligently study in order to pass the citizenship test of their adopted country.

Europeans and other First-worlders outrank Americans in surveys about international affairs. Survey authors attribute the disparity to our large underclass, immigrant populations, and other factors such as market-driven media programming and decentralized education systems. U.S. citizens with the highest incomes fared best on the citizenship test, as did men when compared to women. We might ask, Is there is any good news to be had from this research?

Good news and bad news: Researchers assessed the above survey results and found that these poor scores didn't reflect a lack of intelligence on the part of Americans, but a lack of information, which means people can become more informed *if they make an effort.* The downside is that many don't feel they can spare the time and energy to seek information about how things work: the gears and pulleys of our federal government, various influences upon the national budget, America's overseas interests, the U.S. Constitution, and so forth.

This applies, too, to acquiring and comparing information about religious beliefs. A different survey (from the year prior) showed that Christian believers scored worse than non-believers and followers of other faiths when asked to match the name of a sacred text to its corresponding world religion. Gaining even the most rudimentary information about other cultures, how people live, and what they believe, takes seeking, listening, reading, paying attention, and critical thought.

If only organized religion functioned more like the philosophical and scientific clubs fancied by the eighteenth century deist, philosopher, inventor, and statesman—Benjamin Franklin. He gravitated to what he called "juntos," essentially groups of like-minded people with common interests, but who practiced inquiry, discussion, and debate, not strict adherence to a single dogmatic viewpoint. It was a period now known as The Enlightenment, a time of openness to thoughtful inquiry and a searching out of answers to those questions deemed of public import.

Franklin believed in a benevolent creator who took a hands-off approach, but he rarely attended church. He loved civil discourse and the written word, and was all for figuring out the workings of the world around him, tinkering, questioning, experimenting, and he always wanted to hear what others had to say. A pragmatist who espoused compromise, he adjusted his own views when another's seemed more rational.

The Enlightenment is long over, and in some regards we are poorer for it. I wonder where we now might find believers practicing inquiry and debate, examining the natural sciences, philosophy, world religions, human-ism, atheism, and other perspectives? Where does criti-cal thinking come into play when it's so convenient to follow organized religion's directives regarding how to act, who to wage war against, what amount of sexuality is acceptable, which marital partner commands the oth-er, how to dress, in short—not only how to behave, but how to think about how to behave.

Leaving the thinking to others is, well, easy. Sure, it would take effort to expand our civic knowledge and our understanding of not just our own culture but oth-ers. But it would ultimately yield a more resilient, wiser populace. The tradeoff: fewer beers with the boys in front of big-screen Monday Night Football games, and fewer afternoons spent wandering the mall in search of that just-right pair of kitten heels. We could do it. We could become better informed, more well-rounded peo-ple. If we wanted to.

In other news—in December 2010, a *USA Today* story reported on two recent surveys that "nine in 10 Ameri-cans celebrate Christmas, even if they're atheists, agnostics, or believe in non-Christian faiths such as Judaism and Islam." The surveys, conducted by LifeWay Research and *USA Today*/Gallup, found that six in ten respondents encouraged belief in the Christ component of Christmas, and three in ten read the Biblical story of Christmas.

The director of LifeWay described it as a "head nod" to Jesus by people who "spend time and dime pleasing themselves." Methinks the director sounds unhappy, not with the majority who report believing in Christ+Christmas, but with the percentage who help malls instead of churches meet their overhead. He might be reading too much into the survey numbers.

Such surveys inevitably include respondents who are Christians in name only. There must be plenty of people who think of themselves as Christians but who don't actually *practice*, at least not in the manner preferred by church authorities. They were taught Christianity and know the motions, but the Bible? They're just not that into it. Perhaps some folks like the *idea* of believing without all the requisites. When it comes to verbalizing a position, they default to Christianity. How easy it is to assert an oft-repeated position, whether deeply held or not. We all do it. We go with the flow and conform to what others endorse. Our answers assume the contours of family traditions or cultural ties because those long-held notions, though permeable, don't budge without a fight. And that stranger posing the survey questions? He won't know just what we mean when we fudge the answers. When it comes to counting believers, some of those counted actually count in name only.

During that same holiday season mentioned above, a package from my mother brought me a syndicated

newspaper comic strip called "Mallard Fillmore" which
ran "a message of Christian faith and blessings to all
those who believe, especially those who are persecuted
for believing." The character of Mallard Fillmore is a
duck and he delivered the message. In that same package came a holiday newspaper ad for Scheels, a sporting
goods retailer. The Scheels ad bore an illustration of the
nativity scene: Joseph, Mary, baby Jesus. The headline
"He is born" floated above. Below were remarks attributed to Ronald Reagan:

> In spite of everything, we Americans are still
> uniquely blessed, not only with the rich bounty of
> our land but by a bounty of spirit — a kind of year-
> round Christmas spirit that still makes our country
> a beacon of hope in a troubled world and that
> makes this Christmas and every Christmas even
> more special for all of us who number among our
> gifts the birthright of being an American.

I appreciate the quote, especially since the term
"Christmas spirit" connotes a generic message of sharing
and goodwill. There is something quirky, though, about
the amalgam of a sporting goods retailer, a nativity scene, and The Gipper in a Christmas advertisement. That
combination strikes me as uniquely American.

My friend Carol W says that religion seems to be for
people who are afraid of death, that religions formed to
provide beliefs about there being something after this
life. People become so used to each day following the
last that they can't imagine life ending and that the end
might really be The End. She says that people want
something else after this life ceases.

Carol, born on December 25, explored churches and religion in her early years, though her family was non-religious. Eventually she visited services at an Episcopal church. Now when Christmas Eve approaches, she hungers for a traditional midnight mass, "the pomp and ceremony" of it, the carols and incense. She loves taking communion, "even though I don't know what for, I just love it." She doesn't attend at any other time, doesn't belong to a church, perhaps doesn't even believe. She's one of the many whose actions incite the displeasure of the aforementioned director of LifeWay, but I've been with her to midnight mass on Christmas Eve and it puts a smile on her face like few other things do.

During the same month of my conversation with Carol an Episcopal church in Reno closed—St. Stephen's, which had operated for forty-five years. The Reno Gazette-Journal cited St. Stephen's shrinking congregation and the poor economy. Bishop Dan Edwards reportedly told his congregation to look forward, and to move forward in God's work. I have to think that as congregations age, natural attrition takes place at the very moment when young people embrace other social, non-religious ways to connect with others in a globally integrated world. Perhaps churches, like other businesses, need to evolve into other economically-relevant forms, or else modernize and personalize the way they deliver their messages. I picture the three hundred worshipers at Calvary's early service. Three hundred is a good-sized crowd. And as this memoir goes to press, southwest Reno's Lutheran Church of the Good Shepherd is expanding.

14
Breathing Under Water

I t's not that church matters of my youth held no
interest for me at all. At about the age of twelve I
was platonically smitten with one of our pastor's
sons. My memory assigns him the name of John, or
maybe Jack. Older than me by a few years, he may have
been sixteen, or twenty, or any other number on the opposite shore of the moat sheltering my life. He was utterly out of reach.

Boys, I knew: my brothers and their friends—noisy,
stinky, busy, arms flung wide to the world, not entirely
foreign, but of some rare genus, *masculinous obscurous*
or the like. Thus my attraction to a creature both famil-
iar and strange, and never the thought that a dark-
haired specimen must necessarily joke and sweat and
piss to a melody similar to the blond brother-songs of
my every day. I simply gazed at the pastor's son from a
distance.

Loitering in the shadows of my attraction to the pastor's son was my sense that such a creature might be in
training for the pulpit, potential future preacher and
shepherd of a flock desirous of yet more sheep. Notwithstanding that he was beyond me for other reasons,
on the matter of faith a fog rose up and I knew the moat

between us was unbreachable. When the fog burned off, my Christian beliefs would still hang in shreds.

Church held other phenomena. For instance, one Sunday when I was nine or ten, an unusual effect came over me as I sat with my mother and brothers. There was the minister, tall and sure, at the pulpit atop the central podium. The words he spoke rose perfectly formed in the warm air, but for some reason they formed first in my head, as if I were hearing them an instant before they reached my ears. These were not advance thoughts about the sermon's intent or theme, not the Reverend's brainwaves either, just the words leaving the O of his mouth while forming simultaneously inside my head.

An unsettled feeling came over me. I wasn't afraid. Rather, I observed myself observing him while trying to determine just what was happening. Was I imagining this? It seemed not. Was there something about this particular day that might account for these mental atmospherics? Not that I could detect. I sat very still, certain that this strange and eerie effect was a solitary occurrence. There was no need to explain it to others, since how in the world could it be explained? I had no reason to think it would ever recur.

But recur it did, for perhaps a dozen Sundays, beckoning sermons in stereo, a transmitter inside the pastor's head sending to my head a stream of dreamy, linked words about God's plan for humanity, the fallibility of humans, and the spirit endowed in each of us.

I lack a perfect recall of those sermons, but I can guess their general themes based on the many I heard throughout the years. Methodists don't do fire and brimstone, just sober Christian concepts. For a few months my stereo brain-receiver thwarted my absorption of any content of those sermons.

Perhaps it was a trick of pre-adolescence, or an overactive imagination, or some warp in the time-space continuum that happened to catch upon my personal frequency and of all the people in the world, I was briefly able to discern it. Maybe I was sulking about being forced into attending church each week and my creativity was conjuring up an interesting diversion through a counter-focusing of auditory signals. Or maybe it was my budding contrariness emerging first in a church-shaped setting. As it was, the special effect continued until eventually it petered out of its own accord. It was not a sign from God. It did not portend the arrival of special spiritual knowledge, because that the same phenomenon also blinked to life during the television news my father dialed up in the evenings. It wasn't about faith at all.

Something else I practiced while church services proceeded around me was a type of internal standoff against assertions and commands being issued from the pulpit. During a Methodist service of the 1960s it was common for the pastor to pray aloud in addition to delivering Bible lessons and a sermon. Inevitably there would be sayings to the effect, "We humble ourselves before His almighty power," to which I would state silently, "No I don't." Or if it was, "The Lord is my shepherd," I'd internalize the opposite, "No. He's not." At the time it felt like one way to test the teachings, like poking a water balloon with my pencil to see what would happen. God was supposed to know our thoughts. If I challenged him silently and no lightning zigged down from the sky, perhaps he wasn't there after all.

Lest you think I have no use for churches, I will state categorically that churches can be some of the most traditionally handsome buildings in any town. I married my husband at the corner of First and West streets in a historic stone church embellished with stained glass windows and patinaed pews that glow in the low light. We belonged to no church and in our fourteen months together had never spoken about religion, but I had been inside that place and admired its innate beauty, the jewel-like window above the altar, the lovely woodwork, and, I'll admit, while there I felt echoes of the churches I knew in my childhood.

If you're going to stage a performance, a church embodies the perfect design, with seats facing a raised platform. Since a wedding is a performance staged with props, music, and costumed people speaking rehearsed parts, what better venue than a church? Frankly, I would have married my husband anywhere—in a graveyard, in an alley, on a ditch bank—but we had the choice of an artfully grand place that would also shelter us from the weather; the church was available for a fee. The pastor used a few God-words in our ceremony, but no matter. Our wedding photos captured all the beauty.

In years past, just being in a church could make me want to cry. This was after those early years of Sunday services with my mother, during which I silently sulked about being forced to attend (my discomfort did not merit tears just then). I refer to the intervening years after my youth but before I came out about my atheism. So it was that I'd be in a church during a wedding, a funeral, or a christening, and certain prayers or Bible readings might bring me to the verge of tears. I'd think, "What? What is this about?"

Maybe it was that weddings and funerals are natural well-points of emotion, all those tears of happiness for others, or tears of sorrow and loss. But what about those occasions that weren't weddings or funerals? Rare, yes, but looking back I'm sure it happened.

Was it that I felt hypocritical about reciting the Lord's Prayer along with everyone else around me? It seemed that silence would call attention to my unwillingness to go along with the crowd, and I had been raised to cooperate. Cooperate I did, while knowing that praying wasn't for me, that I was acting the part of willing participant while disbelieving the words. More likely it was an internalized sympathy for all the people who believed a creator was listening and would bless them for their faith, when I felt just the opposite—that those beliefs would go unanswered.

A few years ago I explained my non-believing status to my mother, who considers herself "born again." We have only in recent years conversed about topics of import: aging, marriage, sex, infirm parents, my father, politics. Not religion, though. We still don't discuss her theology or my lack thereof, and I suspect she cannot bear the thought of standing eye-to-eye while my mouth disclaims her God. She is Christian through and through, but she doesn't overtly sell it. Instead, she drops references into conversation, the merest mentions of having lain awake after finishing her prayers, or finally getting a broadcast signal for a Christian television station carrying a program that sometimes includes a group of singing brothers.

I am fairly certain she assumed her children were Christians to one degree or another, though it would have been hard to tell through observation alone. Perhaps religion is such an emotional, highly personal subject for her that it seems akin to talking about sex—almost taboo.

I came out to my mother about my disbelief while speaking into a mini-recorder. That's how we exchanged letters for fifteen years or more—recording our spoken accounts describing work, shopping, flower gardening, bits about fashion, the minutia of the day-to-day (now we phone or email each other). We would exchange the tapes by mail, and when we played them, there would be the voice of the person who lived a thousand-plus miles away.

While navigating northern California in the vicinity of Lake Almanor, I spoke my truth into the recorder, revealing what I had carried hidden inside me for all those years. I suppose I could no longer bear the thought of half-pretending, or pseudo-believing, or whatever the label is for that limbo place where you find yourself unable to contradict someone, who by receiving the particulars will likely be hurt.

An evergreen forest of dappled light formed itself around slices of tall blue sky and crystalline air beyond my car window, forming the sort of day that induces in me a sensation of almost flying and a yearning to drive without ever reaching a destination.

I palmed the recorder and explained that since we never talked about religion it may have seemed that we were in concert, she and I, yet we weren't. I spoke my truth about not believing in God, but in people, in humanity's fallibility and its promise. How important it seems to live a good life today and tomorrow, *for* today and tomorrow, not for the securing of some future payoff such as Christ's second coming, or an E-ticket to

Heaven. I also said that I respect other people's beliefs and their need to believe, and that I recognize that others seek comfort from a higher power, even if I don't always understand why, even if such choices are not for me.

My words flowed. I was buoyed by the spicy bite of pine in the air, and the heady independence that overcomes me when I'm on the road. I set aside the half-completed tape when I arrived at my destination and finished it during my return trip home.

As luck would have it, I mailed that tape but it arrived unplayable on my mother's end, its case broken from rough handling by the postal people. She emailed me to say it had caught in her tape player and become a tangled mess. She wouldn't have known what deep declarations had been lost.

I re-recorded the news of my irreligiousness, trying to recapture the phrasings that had seemed so right the first time. It didn't have the same sparkle as words uttered alongside a glorious forest in spring, words spoken from a high wire without a safety net, but it would do the job. I knew she'd be disappointed, and that my revelation would have the effect of causing yet more praying on her part. She would now need to pray for my errant soul.

If I remember right, she expressed surprise and a little disappointment, which she recorded on the next tape she sent my way. But no lectures or the voicing of fears for my afterlife. In the months to follow she increasingly sent me clippings of stories with references to the greatness of God, or someone crediting God for the paramedics' speedy response, or a child's inspired call to 9-1-1 when a house caught fire. She was trying to show me that others believe in God, which of course I know. *I know.*

When I disclosed this research project for my next novel, how I was visiting churches and talking to people about Heaven, my mother said that the resulting story would interest her more than my first novel, which she had declined to read because it stars a young woman who hitchhikes into trouble. I imagine she thinks that a story that includes church or Heaven will be a gentler, sweeter read, but I'm not prepared to promise it will work out quite that way.

To my knowledge, my mother hasn't attended church regularly in years, except for one time two years ago when she accompanied me to a service for the sake of research. Perhaps her abstinence has spanned all the years since she and my father divorced. Or maybe, having relocated to her birthplace, she dabbled at attending before deciding it didn't any longer suit her. For one thing, church people ask questions and want to be sociable, and the church wants your name and phone number in order to reach out and invite you to Bible study or some other gathering. They want information she's not willing to share (so she said), so she doesn't go to church but instead worships God in her own way at home, praying and reading one of her many Bibles.

According to an October 2010 news story on ABC News, my mother's home worship aligns with the six-to-nine million Americans who worship in what are called "home churches," literally private homes serving as worship places for small groups of like-minded believers. That research only counts groups, not single individuals who eschew traditional churches in favor of private prayer, so my mother is one of the singletons who was not counted. Come to think of it, the grandfather of Ashtyn-from-Mustang, who taught the family from the Bible at home—his would have been one of those home churches.

The reported six-to-nine million home worshipers represent 12% of Americans identified as religious, and that number is probably growing as more people desire the connection to other believers but want an intimate setting with fewer trappings, ceremony, and dogma. Also smaller expectations of financial support.

In the years since having spoken my personal truth to my mother I haven't once been moved to tears while in church. It feels like being able to breathe under water when I thought I'd forgotten how.

15
A Narrow Path to Salvation,
but Every Good Person Gets In

~~ Our Lady of the Snows Catholic Church ~~

I n early spring I visited Our Lady of the Snows Catholic Church (also known as "Snows"), a church of longstanding in old southwest Reno. I had meant to find a Catholic Church that held a Mass resembling those of the late 1950s or early 1960s, the timeframe of my novel-to-be. In the 1950s the service would have been in Latin, and head coverings required for female parishioners. Both those practices, though, were retired in the 1960s.

As I approached the brick church house on a brisk March day, I crossed paths with two different women, and each greeted me with a smile and a simple "hello." Already the place felt friendly. I took a seat in the farthest right back pew, the better to observe most of the large, bright room and its congregation; also cover for how I meant to take notes. From that spot I could hear two women posted near the doors behind me. There came laughter and the sounds of people arriving as one woman said, "We're the greeters." The place began to fill up.

From the holder attached to the back of a pew I pulled a book labeled *DAILY MASS PROPERS ~ Breaking*

Bread. The March 7 Daily Mass provided choices and options for readings, one being Proverbs 31:30, 28 Entrance: "Honor the woman who fears the Lord. Her sons will bless her, and her husband praise her."

The sanctuary was painted cream and brown with large stained-glass windows depicting St. Anne, Jesus and the Children, St. Joseph, and three others, all softly aglow from the overcast day. Four sections of angled pews faced a raised marble platform and alter. Decorations seemed plentiful: a carved crucified Christ hung on the front wall, vibrant green topiary in pots, large flower arrangements, various statuary and artworks, a poster marking the progress of fundraising pledges for the parish's parochial school expansion project. A colorful forest green cloth draped the altar. Nearby stood carved wooden screens. The *DAILY MASS PROPERS* identified this as "Ninth Sunday in Ordinary Time," the last Sunday before Lent.

A woman lit candles atop tall marble columns at each side of the altar, and one adjacent to the pulpit. Another woman read the greeting (and other Bible lessons during the service). I was glad to see women participating because my understanding is that in times past they were denied a role in Catholic services. Though the Virgin Mary is venerated, women may not hold church positions of authority, by order of the Vatican where the rules are made. I've read that nuns "run" the Papal Household. Skeptic that I am I suspect such "running" likely includes housekeeping and other similar duties.

Broadly speaking, in Christian teachings, women are maligned for causing the "original sin" perpetrated in the Garden of Eden, the first male having been utterly innocent and easily led astray by the evil, cunning first female. Thereafter, half the world's population is tarred with a brush of Biblical origins.

In spite of centuries of institutionalized discrimination, Catholic women might be the most devout believers. I don't know of any research to that effect, but I suspect that women gravitate to organized religion more so than men, which may correlate with women's diminished status, at least in American life.

A recent news report cited one in four U.S. children residing within single-parent families, and the majority of those families as living in poverty (since women still receive almost 30% less in wages than men do for the same work). It makes sense then that we will find women as heads of most single-parent households, and also women targeted more often than men for abuse and family violence. It makes sense that women might seek hope and comfort outside the home and workplace, where economic and social disparities most often occur. Organized religion, which offers spiritual comfort and the promise of a more golden afterlife, might represent a natural choice, an easy choice, even though religions based on Old Testament principals dismiss and defame women, and Catholicism and Islam withhold from women the chance to lead others in worship. They seem to be promoting women as only followers, never as leaders.

Didn't more men attend church throughout centuries past than do now? I don't know the exact numbers, but back when church membership was associated with sound thinking and a necessity for garnering influence, men led the parade to chapel. Now it seems that politics and church membership remain the primary spheres where attention to religion accrues merit points.

I'd bet my next ice cream cone that the shift of men away from church attendance parallels the rise of televised sports in America (maybe across the globe). Once television stole radio's thunder, it monopolized sports, eventually spawning networks dedicated to sports and sporting events; today we can even get them streamed to a laptop, pc, tablet, or smart phone. Does that explain why men come from Mars but not from church? Maybe.

Perhaps men have become worshipers at the Church of Sports. Rather than emulating Biblical figures they can live vicariously through athletes, wearing copies of their uniforms and talking their talk, communing with others through cheering, shouting, and cursing instead of conversation, prayer, and contemplation. Best of all, being a casual fan (the kind I am) requires little thought or effort—simply choose an athlete or team and take a seat. No memorization required, no training, no election, you need not learn the lingo. Just ask me and I'll tell you how a baseball stadium is a sparkling place on a summer night, a mass of infectious energy, and how a Polish dog is a thing of beauty when consumed to the roar of a hometown crowd.

I would caution observers not to mistake the enthusiasm of fans. Fans don't *care* about a particular athlete or team. They don't root for a quarterback, a starting pitcher, or a power forward with the thought that he should do well because success will make him a better citizen and family man. They don't reason how "She crushed that 3-wood. I bet she's trustworthy and is raising her kids to be strong, independent thinkers." Nor do they cheer, "Did you see that f--'n pass? Like a rocket! He's got to be the best volunteer in the NFL." In amateur sports, people rally for their youngster's teams, and there are spouses and family members who cheer for professional athletes because they love them in a familial way. But dyed-in-the-wool damn-the-torpedoes fans seek validation through choosing well, through the *rightness* of being fans. Lacking their own World Series ring, they settle for the occasional high of picking a winner. If fans, male or female, can feel special through sports, they may not seek comfort through church.

And another thing: Social media may be the youngest generations' alternative to church. Through social media, people can choose a tribe of friends to connect with, to share with, to commiserate with. In some ways it's more intimate than the sharing that takes place between congregants in a church. Think: photos with captions detailing a path through life, books read, favorite products, restaurants, the sharing between friends and friends of friends. Facebook as a substitute for church? Could be.

Back to Snows. During a baptism early in the service, Father Tony Vercellone said, "On behalf of the Church I claim this child for God." The parents and godparents each traced the mark of the cross on the baby's forehead. Tiny Molly Diana was baptized to a round of applause. She gazed out at the two hundred-plus watchers, another child introduced to Christianity by parents and the culture into which she was born.

The service's music was fairly traditional. Four women and two men sang. One of the men played a piano. There was call and response:

The word of the Lord.
Praise be to the Lord.
The Lord be with you.
And also with you.

There followed readings from Deuteronomy, Psalms, Romans, and Matthew. Father Tony, wearing forest green vestments, stepped down off the platform to stand in front of the pews. His voice rang with warmth and humor as he spoke of a recent visit to his ninety-three year old father who was recovering from a heart attack and who has some dementia. I thought: I could like Father Tony.

During the sermon Father Tony said that we each are a gift—a son, a daughter of God. That God loves us powerfully. Do we treat each other as gifts? He recounted that Jesus says for us not to be hypocrites (a word deriving from *actor*). Be real. We are gifts to each other and our families, from God. He asked rhetorically: Do you reject Satan? Do you believe in God Almighty, creator of Heaven and earth? Do you believe in Jesus Christ...do you believe in the Holy Spirit?

A group of eight "candidates and catechumens" formed a line in front of the congregation. Candidates are adults who have been baptized in a Christian church. Catechumens are new to the rites of Christian initiation. The church newsletter explained the next steps for these individuals, including a "Rite of Sending" and a symbolic election into the church. The final period of the Rite of Christian Initiation for Adults (RCIA) is the Period of Purification and Enlightenment, which per Snows' newsletter "closes the period of the Catechumenate proper, that is the lengthy period of formation of the catechumens' minds and hearts."

I've been told that communion is held during every Catholic mass. Snows' communion featured polished silver bowls and chalices. Father Tony was attended by two acolytes, one girl and one boy, and assisted by both women and men. Next came the Lord's Prayer spoken aloud. All around me parishioners grasped their neighbor's hands. To my right stood a soprano who had sung the earlier hymns without consulting a hymnal. Facing forward, she held her hands aloft—invitation to a stranger, no insult if declined. I took her hot, damp hand in mine as she prayed aloud. I did not pray, but silently I sent these thoughts down the length of my arm: I take your hand because you are my sister on this earth, a gift to your family and friends.

After the service concluded, I discerned that women were indeed the majority as I had guessed, and on that day most of the crowd looked forty and older. As the congregants filtered out after the service, I spotted someone I hadn't seen in months, a man who runs a local golf course pro shop. He was there with his elderly mother, and greeted me with a hug and a smile. Then I toured the rest of the sanctuary for a closer look at its components. An "Ambry" cabinet held "Oil of the sick," "Oil of the Catechumens," and "Chrism." An alcove was labeled "Food for Life" and held bags of donated foodstuff. On the east wall hung a large photo display of deployed soldiers, sailors, and airmen. The heading at the top read "Make me an instrument of thy Peace. Where there is hatred, let me sow love." Below the photos were these place names: S. Korea, Iraq, Afghanistan, Kuwait.

Dispensers at the back of the sanctuary held Holy Water. There was a tri-level fixture of blue glass votives and candles. A few folks lingered in the aisles, visiting. Father Tony strode past dressed in street clothes, most likely headed toward the next commitment on his busy Sunday calendar. In fact, the Snows newsletter listed a roster of weekend and weekday masses, Adoration of the Blessed Sacrament, Reconciliation, Holy Days of Obligation, Civic Holiday Masses, Communion to the Homebound, details on arranging Baptisms and Marriages, Holy Orders, Anointing of the Sick, First Holy Communion and Confirmation, and RCIA. There were scripture study classes and auxiliary meetings, a breakfast club, a prayer group, a senior art class, a benefit concert, details about observing Lent, and more. One feature highlighted Theology on Tap, a "forum for young adults to learn about and discuss their faith in a relaxing social setting," to be held at a local barbecue restaurant. The parish staff for Snows numbered seventeen strong.

Near the back of the church I notice Smitty, a self-described convert to Catholicism from Southern Methodism. He stands near his wife who is conversing with someone else. I had not realized that they attend Snows. Smitty greets me, saying, "I see you're taking notes."

I explain my research and how I want to get the details right. He offers to answer any questions, so I ask what he thinks Heaven will be like. He pauses a moment before saying it will be "Pleasant all around. No one higher or lower, all the same."

I must ask: Not even God will be higher? He grants that he means all will be equal except for God and Jesus being above the rest.

Might Heaven hold only Catholics? He says it will include all manner of people, Muslims and Pygmies too.

So they wouldn't have to believe in the Catholic way? He thinks not. They will need to have lived a good life, which can be accomplished without even being a Christian. He's been a Christian all his life, though, and the longer he lives the more he realizes how narrow seems the path to salvation. "You sin and then you go to confession and then the next week you sin some more and you go to confession again." He shakes his head as if pondering a monumental task.

As I type the above reference to confession I am reminded of the Catholic Church's sex-abuse scandals and the exodus of many members in response. My understanding of sexual abuse is that its perpetrators are most often adults in positions of authority, particularly those whom children and parents consider trustworthy (naturally, they're the ones with access to children). In nuclear and blended families it's most often the father or stepfather. Not that mother's aren't physical and emotional abusers; they are. But they sexually abuse children less often than do men. Amazingly, it's a given organization's or family's figureheads, nurturers, role models, and mentors who prove deviant. How ironic then that it's been Fathers (the term for Catholic priests) misusing their positions to injure children. *Father*, as in "I'll protect and provide for you, steering you toward the future with a steady hand." *Father*, as in, "Trust me."

I suspect that if not for a few brave victims who finally broke the code of silence and shame, nary a word would have escaped the Church itself about its own Fathers' sins. This whole scandal makes me glad not to be Catholic. Not because of the individual abusers, though I wish for them all to know the inside of prisons. What most curdles my good will is the manner by which the Church's hierarchy first covered up the scandal then downplayed its seriousness. For too long they acted the part of royalty, at a remove from the petty concerns of the injured, whose ilk have for millennia enriched Church coffers, financing its treasure houses of artwork and antiquities, its jeweled vestments and gilded cathedrals. I do admire the few priests who have spoken out against these abusers, and the dioceses which have apologized to victims and attempted reparations.

These days I wonder who heard abuser-Fathers' confessions and absolved them of such sins? Over the years, individuals within the hierarchy provided absolution and allowed some offenders to continue as priests. How many Hail Marys and Our Fathers constituted sufficient penance for a single act of molestation, or a dozen? How many for sodomy? For rape? Imagine a perpetrator's relief at facing not a victim, the person wronged (as would be expected in Judaism), but someone at a distance from the act itself who could assuage the offender's perverted sense of entitlement.

And if absolution has been granted those abuser-priests, do they get a shot at admission to Heaven? Do they have as good a chance at passing through purgatory and into the line at the pearled gates as say, an ordinary sinner accompanying his wife to church on a Sunday?

In Christian Science every human passes to the other side regardless of his or her life on Earth. Murderers, rapists, atheists, everyone, not to a shining city in the clouds, but to some other existence.

I know what a prime example I am of human failings. For instance, let the evidence show how unforgiving I can be. I harbor a deep ill will toward all abusive clergy as well as toward those who drove the getaway car or provided any perpetrators with safe haven. Even if I believed in an afterlife I would not want to share an iota of space or energy or a divine state of mind with any child-abusing priests. Put me on a different escalator. I wouldn't go anywhere with them.

In contrast, here is dear Smitty's thoughtful smile and genteel manner as he muses about the difficulties of trying to navigate a straight path, how much effort and attention it takes, with no promise of making the grade come Judgment Day, a church-going father/ husband/ son giving regular thought to salvation and Heaven, and as far as I can tell, not abusing a single person along the way. If anyone were to gain heavenly admission, wouldn't it be someone who spends time and energy working toward salvation, someone who doesn't give up trying but tries and tries again?

Any recollection of my own father attending church eludes me. No faint outline of him at my mother's side, no watery recollection, not a one, though this could be the faulty spark plugs of my memory shorting out. Perhaps he attended our baptisms. From across many decades the details go missing.

I am sure he attended various weddings and funerals, which in those days commonly took place in a church whether the participants were members or not, but that would have been propriety at play. He never interfered with my mother's pursuit of faith, or her insistence that her children participate.

My father was darkly handsome, cool-tempered, and blessed with a voice that the microphone loved. A slight man, he seemed somehow larger than other fathers. Though he wrote and recorded commercials and was a respected radio and television broadcaster, it was decades later that I learned about his aspirations to writing stories and songs for publication. All those years later, too, I learned of his infidelities.

While my brothers and I were tricycling about, our father had been unfaithful to my mother, and by extension to us. To keep him from leaving my mother had reasserted her love for him and their children's need of a father. She argued that he would lose his children's affection and respect, and convinced him that child support payments for four dependents would prove steep. I imagine my father recalled how he had lived for a time in a children's home when his own parents divorced. My mother prevailed and my father stayed.

Now I wonder why he skipped virtually every Sunday service at my mother's religious haven on Florin Road. Was he agnostic, or atheist? Or was he simply avoiding that which she desired and enjoyed, in the process maintaining an emotional distance from the woman he had once planned to leave.

By the time we were teenagers my mother worked outside our home. Her job at a military depot surrounded her with many workmates and friends. When she could no longer take my father's remoteness, she heeded the pull of the world beyond her tepid marriage and divorced him. At that point my father developed a desire to hold on. I have letters written from him to her, in pencil, ballpoint ink, and black felt pen on the yellow legal paper he used for business. In what appears to be his first, reduced here to bones, the hurting roles had reversed:

Dear ---,
Easy, up front expression of feelings is not my long suit.
You may have noticed.

I don't "talk too good" when the subject is me. Not the real me—the inner me. The me that nobody sees. The private, secret, sensitive me.

I wondered, often, just when it is a man begins to grow that shell—when he finally agrees to live by the code "big boys don't cry"... when he decides to be ever stoic. The months and years of that thickening of skin are logged by the months & years of learning to cope with other men—of sorting out the who you are from the who you're going to be and the who you wish you were.

....

You've seen nothing of what I've written for some years now. That's the private me that no one knows. The naked, bare, defenseless me. The me I've never learned to trust you with, because it's the one that can be hurt.

I'd love to be able to share that with you and have it understood.

Not evaluated.

Not judged.

Not criticized.

Just understood.

....

Constant work is not really a "high."

....

I struggled long hours for lots of years to polish the skills I have. But after I've put in my day, there are lots of things I'd rather do. I'd rather go fishing than mow a lawn. I'd rather read a good book than pull cables in the attic. I'd rather lay on my back and stare at the sky than clean out a chicken house, or wash dishes, or clean out the refrigerator, or

weed the garden, or paint the house, or fix the gate,
or reset the mailbox post, or stain shutters or prune
the trees or haul garbage to the dump.

I'd rather make love than fight about money. Even
on Sunday.

....

All my love,
Me

In this letter my father invokes only the two of them
and their inexorable drift, and the hopes he has of bail-
ing their sinking boat fast enough to reach shore before
the whole thing collapses. In a later missive he invokes
God by name, just once, but I wonder now if it was
simply his own personal anguish that made him write,
"God knows I don't want to lose you." Just that one reference. It strikes me now that when faced with losing
my mother, my father may have found himself a step
closer to wanting a God he could turn to, one that might
bless his newly-restored desire for fidelity in marriage.

It is sometimes said that during the terrible pressures
of waging war against other humans, and while faced
with their own mortality, soldiers sometimes develop a
need for God. Maybe others do too—husbands and
wives, friends and lovers. Maybe life's battles bring people close enough to the brink of disbelief in themselves
that they look outward for a beacon. Or maybe my father thought a reference to my mother's God would sof-
ten the stone he had planted in her heart.

I cannot recall my father ever emoting in person the
way he writes in these letters, the lines reading like life-
blood splayed out on a page. But too, my father, a writ-
er-for-hire, understood the seduction of evocative prose.
It's crafted to make a person believe. A small black shard

at the center of me wonders whether he wrote without wholly meaning what his words seem to convey. I'd like to think he contained such depth of emotion, even though that would mean he harbored unrequited dreams and an abiding pain expressed too late.

After my parents divorced, my mother quit her church, the one from my childhood. She tells me now that she doesn't remember saying this, but I recall her concern that certain people there would be judgmental about her divorce and she couldn't bear to be around them if they looked askance at her new circumstances. They might have, and she may have known them well enough to assume the worst. In any event, she gave up the physical church. But she never stopped believing in the power of God to sustain her.

My father later died, too young. His then-wife arranged his cremation. The memorial service took place in an auditorium, neutral territory. A number of his old friends and workmates said nice things about the finest of his qualities and talents. I don't recall any prayers.

Forgive us, California, but six months later we kids, tethered to lives stretching in opposite directions, came from disparate cities across the West for the scattering of Dad's ashes upon the June waters of his favorite fishing stream. We stood on the rocks below a bridge I now think of as "Dad's bridge." It was not a primo fishing hour (when bugs hatch—early morning or else at dusk), but there we were. I don't recall much conversation, just a few unrehearsed thoughts spoken aloud. There was little reason to speak about that which he himself had left unsaid.

When ashes drift out onto moving water they vanish into eddies, riffles, and the shadows where willows

overgrow the water. The dust of him was gone before
tears could come. We stood on the rocky bank, swallow-
ing against dry throats.

A healthy waterway teams with life: fish eggs and
minnows, ill-fated water skippers and drunken mayflies
felled by a summer breeze. Catch one wing and the surface will pull you under. Larvae and worms, algae and
things that beg a microscope. Submerged grasses along
the banks reach through the rush toward the watery
light above. And the non-living: sand and sediment,
flakes of mica and gold, and stones turned and smooth-
tumbled, slicked by the stream's mossy tongue.

My own imagining of what happened goes like this:
Downstream in a pool where the current slows, the surface shimmered with pale flecks resembling the pollen
of nearby Jeffrey pines. A rainbow trout flicked its tail
and took the bait—the intake of dust, the outflow, and
the inexorable slow drift to the bottom. Not quite dust
to dust, but the culmination of a long passage from an
ocean's murky depths to the weedy bed of a mountain
stream. I like to think it happened that way. It could
have.

Fifteen years or so after my father's death, Mother
confided how had she known she would spend so many
years alone she might have done things differently. She
might have chosen to stay with my father. Maybe. Not
long ago she had copies made from an original photo of
my father taken the year they married. On the back of
the print she sent to me, her declaration in flourishes of
black ink: "1952. The wonderful man I married."

16
The "A" Word

I have been talking to friends and acquaintances, and a few strangers too, about their religious beliefs. Since these are all people I can easily reach out to they're not a random sample, not even do friends-of-friends count as random. But they're all people who when asked have agreed to share their views.

We are sitting in a camp at the base of a mountain range along a high desert valley in northern Nevada when Mike P tells me that he doesn't believe in God or Heaven. "We [humans] are the same as animals on this earth. Dust to dust." To his mind, organized religion serves a purpose; many people need it. He sees religion as a means for "explaining life and death." But he says that science knows more about how life started and how it ends. Religions have done a lot of "harm in the world." He seems to be suggesting that people have used religious beliefs to justify their destruction of others. He scans the scenery around us. "This is my church," he says, gesturing toward the stretch of sage and scrub sloping outward for miles.

Mike tells people he's agnostic because labeling himself an atheist draws odd looks. I understand. Atheism is a word that's all elbows. We make it easier on others and on ourselves when we use soft-cornered words.

The morning Mike and his wife leave camp for home, the sun breaks pink and orange through a scrim of high clouds. Distant alfalfa fields morph from black to green as the night shadows lift, the day gaining color in every direction. It seems a proper setting for the exit of a man who doesn't believe it gets any better than this.

My husband does not buy into a God who sent his only son to be sacrificed for mankind, though he says there may have been a man known as Jesus who was called the son of God. He notes that there is much about life and the universe that seems to suggest intelligent design, that some entity may have placed the elements so that humans could evolve. He can't quite decide if perhaps, maybe, it happened that way.

He does, however, believe in fate. How else could he and I have found each other decades ago after forgoing the many others we each encountered, all the co-workers and business contacts, all the blind dates? And how can one explain the classified ad that proffered our first family dog, a hunter so regal and handsome that people stopped us on the street to ask if he was available for breeding? And then later, as we grieved our first dog's death, how was it that our second became available for adoption?

Even I use the word fate with a casualness that I don't intend as anything other than luck, or some weird collision of coincidence and need. But to my husband, fate means predetermination, that he and I were *meant* to meet and fall in love, and *meant* to own first Mac, and then Pete. That we are sometimes *meant* to be lucky, or smart, or more aware, or to seize an opportunity. He also says, how could that be, when of course we each have choices, and each make choices, and make a dozen choices every day? Are we to think that the fact of those specific choices and then each of their results are predetermined? Are we really just acting out parts of life's play previously written?

If that is the case, our friend was meant to get breast cancer, which she would then subdue with chemicals and diet, and she was meant to have it return years later to threaten her life. She was meant to have not only that struggle but also unceasing worry about the effects of her illness and its outcome upon her young children and devoted family.

Per my husband, the world's workings "can't be just random chance, or happenstance." It seems to him that we humans have intelligence and choice, the wherewithal for decisions, and that sometimes *something* puts us in a position to choose that which is for the best. He says, "We know right from wrong and it's not all that hard to choose wrong." But we get the option of a good choice too. "Somebody up there steered" him to me so that we could choose one another. When I ask if he means a sentient being he says, "I don't know. Maybe. It's not a firm belief, more an intuition" that something makes good things happen. But he concedes that such a perspective cannot account for the Hitlers and Stalins of the world, and Viet Nam, and genocide.

Nor, I will add, can it account for my great-nephew's malfunctioning pulmonary arteries, or his need for a liver transplant at the tender age of three years old. Those I would chalk up to poor luck.

Then there's Peg R, a petite mother of two and instructor of pet first aid classes (yes, there is such a thing). She

answers to Peggy and Peg and an affectionate nickname
that her friends and husband use. At one time she was
one of the busiest volunteer pet adoption facilitators
around.

Peg attended Catholic school for a number of years,
where "things were black and white. You were going to
Hell or Heaven." The rules included "Be obedient, no
lying, confess your sins. Once you confessed you were
absolved." But though the students were not to take the
Lord's name in vain, adults swore all the time. Her
mother swore: "Mary and Joseph!" or, "God damn it!"

Peg believes in Christianity. "I do believe. I think the
person I am today is because of Catholic school, which
gave us manners. You're taught respect for elders." By
contrast, public school looked like a free-for-all. She and
her classmates wore uniforms, which made all the kids
look the same. "It was a hard place to be an individual."
She remembers a fifth-grade spelling bee wherein students had to pronounce the word being spelled. After
she spelled a word in one of the semi-final rounds she
lost by mispronouncing it.

She says, "I remember knowing at a very young age
that going to confession was absolving my sins. All it
bought me was another week, until the next Sunday,
and knowing I was pretty much the same kid. Said my
one hundred Hail Marys. Maybe it made *him* feel better,
thinking I'd be a better kid."

Holiday masses were "wonderful." She loved the singing, felt uplifted by it. "My singing is flawless in church."
But there were five kids scrambling to get to church on
time. Even with bobby-pinning Kleenexes to the girls'
hair, her family was perpetually late. They'd end up in

the leftover seats, the ones right up front, or in the sin-
gles scattered throughout.

About Heaven: Peg's all for it. "It would be the greatest place to be. But I never really thought that, was never in a hurry to get there." Heaven is a reward, "fluffy
and comfortable and stress-less and perfect. All ice
cream sundaes and cartoons. To get there you had to be
the best kid. I was not going to get there. I challenged
everything ... almost challenging God or Heaven. Purgatory was more likely." All that sinning and confessing
and always asking why.

"As you get older," Peg says, "you realize Heaven is
not that carefree. I want it to be more like the Rainbow
Bridge." By that she means the prose poem that describes an ideal pet Heaven. That's where she hopes to
end up. "I don't want to be up there with all those people. I'd rather be with all the pets."

She doesn't expect to get to choose who else will be
in Heaven, but she's hoping it will be categorized for
pets to be with pet lovers, and alcoholics will go to their
own section. It will be pain free. Dead people will arrive
at the age they are when they die. Contrary to how some
others picture Heaven, Peg says, "I don't think it should
be perfect."

I ask whether God is out there. Peg says, "God is out
there. He is, or she is—I still don't know what form. An
energy maybe." The Catholic faith teaches adoration and
admiration, which she finds hard to follow. She sees
God as obscure, doesn't give a lot of thought to God because she "wants to pick and choose the things that
worry me." She doesn't pray, but meditates. She church-
hopped for a while because something "was lacking in
my life," but has not yet identified what exactly is miss-

ing. At one point she tried a Lutheran service, but hasn't settled on any one church. Her husband is non-religious, so she probably feels like she's in this alone.

17

A Buffet of Choices and "The Truth"

C indie G is a young mother and businesswoman who describes herself as "ambivalent about the deification of Jesus, or any other man." But she believes in the teachings of Jesus, as she calls them. She also says, "I do believe there is something to the magic of biology, the wonderment of life. I do feel a connection between all things. I don't see why that couldn't be science." She is working her way toward atheism. "I'd like to get there ... atheism has to be the default."

Heaven, to Cindie's mind, is being "simply in the presence of ... little-g god." She imagines god as an energy and Heaven as plugged into that energy. Heaven doesn't come after this life, contains no space and no time. There, the past, future, and present are all at once. She says, "I do believe in an all-powerful, all-knowing" force. She accepts that there are people attuned to other dimensions of awareness and energy. And she's seen miracles. During one, she broke her foot; it was even crooked. A friend laid hands on it and healed her within seconds.

Let me explain that Cindie is not a woo-woo kind of person. She speaks directly and surely about matters of faith and has studied and read widely about world religions and spirituality. She truly believes that the healing of her foot was a miracle. Being a skeptic, however, I asked if she had gone for an X-ray to see where the break had been, in order to, you know, confirm that her foot had actually been fractured. She had not.

More about Heaven: Cindie finds comfort in the concept and says that it will contain our loved ones, but we won't have to wait for them because Heaven is concurrent with today, with this very moment. I think she means that after death we remain in the moment with the living, thus time and space are negated; perhaps the dead are here with us right now. "In my heart of hearts," she says, "I don't believe in Hell, because why would god/God create Hell? And humans have choice. We can choose not to remain [in this life]." She says shedding one's body is not required for going to Heaven. "Maybe that explains love at first sight, or love for our children." She likes religious imagery, displaying many examples in her office.

Cindie was raised a Catholic by parents who taught their children to seek and explore beyond those teachings. In my book, she is one of the lucky ones. How many believers teach their children: *This theology is one of many. Someday you may find another that will suit you better, or you may find that you don't believe at all.* Out of millions of believers, how many teach their children about the alternatives? A handful? If that many.

Cindie followed her parents' advice to seek and explore, attending, for instance, Episcopal worship services, which resembled Catholic services "without the guilt." She sounds wistful when speaking about the liberal rural church of her formative years. She misses "that feeling of belonging." At church she felt loved. She needed that in her life at the time—the connectedness, the feeling of being welcome at any Catholic service. The once-familiar and its rituals still call to her, but she refuses to be labeled a Christian, and given the current state of the Catholic Church will not align with it.

Life lessons attributed to Jesus resonate with Cindie. "So much is known about where he went and what he taught. He changed the world in three days." But, "If I found out tomorrow that Jesus didn't exist, I would still want to live by those teachings." She continues: "Jesus didn't tell people what *not* to do. He only had two rules." Plus, he was a long-haired nomad, which fits the hippy ethics she was raised by.

Another thing: Cindie doesn't believe in absolute morality, absolute right or wrong, or that god/God intervenes. She says that even though she doesn't expect an answer, "in moments of desperation it brings me comfort to ask for help." She views prayer as a type of meditation focused on an accessible answer. "Prayer gives me something to focus on. Meditation just bores me."

The moral values she finds in some Biblical teachings bring to mind the sixth tenet listed in that old Christian Science leaflet I found. It reads, "And we solemnly promise to watch, and pray for that Mind to be in us which was also in Christ Jesus; to do unto others as we would have them do unto us; and to be merciful, just and pure."

Conversing with Cindie is interesting for the same reasons it is with Lisa—her open-mindedness and her purposeful journey to find answers and values to live by. Neither of them insists there is a single way to think or believe, and they grant the likelihood of other valid viewpoints. This perspective doesn't come from adhering blindly to one set of teachings, but from asking and reading and from self-reflection about what they each need in order to feel informed, perhaps to feel whole. As for Cindie, she likes "a buffet of choices."

The aspect of personal choice seems fitting for an American culture of independent do-it-yourselfers. It does refute, though, theologies which claim to illuminate the Only True Path to a creator. For many (perhaps most) Christian-based denominations there is little room for personal interpretation and no buffet of choices. They do not seek to mold a belief system to worshipers' individual needs for comfort and wholeness, instead expecting followers to shape themselves to the teachings of the church.

My understanding is that Christianity was originally a grass-roots movement that eventually took on a variety of forms. In the Middle and Near East where it originated, it was largely an oral tradition and comprised variations that may have vaguely resembled each other. Upon the Roman empire's expansion, church leaders chose which accounts of extant teachings most suited their style of rule over their many conquered peoples. From this sprang an official state-sponsored religion, which was sacrosanct. No questions allowed, Do Not Pass Go. The penalty for not following this purposefully constructed version of Christianity was death.

There are Christians who don't attend church or study the Bible, who have from traditional theologies stripped those aspects which they feel don't suit a modern life. Perhaps those believers more closely align with ancient believers than with those who follow today's church doctrine, especially Catholicism. Maybe such an independent approach accounts for the many lapsed Catholics I've encountered, including not just those who don't buy into organized religion, but also those who no longer believe in a creator-figure.

To my mind, Jewishness, Christian-ness, and Muslimhood represent states of mind *plus* practice. It doesn't seem to me that absent their attendant belief systems they can accurately reference a culture. For instance, though I was raised with my mother's Christian culture I am not a Christian because I do not believe in or practice that theology. It's not the same as saying I'm a Nevadan (a place to reside), or I used to be a dancer but now I am a writer. Religious references are not just states of mind or a frame of reference with links to the past; they are thoughtful, active worldviews inextricably linked to beliefs. To my mind, declaring oneself a Christian means believing that Jesus was the messiah, which necessarily means believing in God, and therefore Heaven. Even if one doesn't actively read scripture or pray or attend church, to be Christian means to believe not just in some unidentified creator, or spirit, or energy, but specifically in Christ and Christianity. Then again, who am I to say?

Humans being what they are, there have always been lapsed believers. And now there appear to be rivers of people moving away from organized religion. Maybe it's the nature of churches that drives people to abandon structured worship, or maybe religion's assertions about there being a magical, mystical creator. Maybe they're put off by stories about resurrection and ascension, Hell, purgatory, and the devil, or that of six billion people in the world there are only 144,000 "chosen ones" (more on that next), and how churches must operate as businesses if they are to survive. Some people may eventually decide that though a church's aura of community offers

comfort and its rituals a sense of joy, though they connect with some of the teachings-minus-the-miracles,
they cannot abide the notion of original sin and its attendant perpetual guilt, nor those church leaders who
hold themselves up as above the law. Maybe that's why
some beliefs lapse entirely while others evolve into
something less-organized but more-personalized. The
evolution and devolution of faith.

Cindie had told me about a serial conversation she
has maintained with a female Jehovah's Witness. As
Cindie's growing family moved from one home to another (four so far) she made a point of letting the Witness know where to find her. After each successive move
the woman reestablished contact. Consequently, they've
grown to be rather fast friends.

On Friday of the week I visited with Cindie, I took a
walk. I've never belonged to a gym or health spa. For
exercise I walk in my neighborhood because I cannot
see driving to a fitness center in order to use a treadmill,
but also, I like to note each season's effect upon the
neighborhood's trees, the blooms emerging in gardens
visible from the street, and to breathe in the soft green
scent of freshly cut lawns. There are homes for sale, bas-
set hounds baying from behind a wire fence, and the
occasional foreign birdsong that draws my gaze to the
canopy overhead.

Here is what happened that Friday, a mid-spring day
with a chill in the air. Advancing down the street opposite me came seven people: three adults, one teen, and
three children. I watched them navigate our aging
neighborhood, where sidewalks fronting some homes
end abruptly in stretches with bare curbs, sensing a
purposefulness to their manner of dress, their quiet

conversation, and the small books they carried. I knew at a glance they must be Jehovah's Witnesses.

We nodded in greeting across two lanes of asphalt. Minutes later, after looping back the other direction, I passed them again, this time on the same side of the street. I slowed my pace as one of the ladies extended a pamphlet, saying, "We won't be finding you at home so would you like one of these?"

The flyer's front page reads: JESUS "TAKES AWAY the SIN of the WORLD." How does he do so? Why is this necessary? How can you benefit? We invite you to find out on Sunday, April 17, 2011." The inside front panel contains this wording:

> John the Baptizer stated that Jesus 'takes away the sin of the world.' (John 1:29) This drew attention to Jesus's role in saving obedient mankind. Why though, did Jesus have to die to save sinners? What did he achieve by willingly giving up his life? Who benefits from his death? What can it mean for you? Each year, Jehovah's Witnesses gather to commemorate Jesus's death on its anniversary. This year, the anniversary falls on Sunday, April 17, after sundown. Jehovah's Witnesses warmly invite you to meet with them to examine the significance of Jesus's death. The Bible's answers to the above questions will be considered.

The pamphlet, printed in soothing green tones, credits the Watch Tower Bible and Tract Society of Pennsylvania, copyright 2011, and cites their website as www.watchtower.org. The right-hand panel shows a Caucasian man at a lectern with a Bible in hand before a diverse audience seated in chairs. Because I knew absolutely nothing about the workings of Jehovah's Witnesses, it seemed I should take advantage of this invitation to a public gathering. And so I did.

On the specified evening in April (listed on my Disabled American Veterans calendar as Passover), I joined roughly three hundred people divided between two meeting rooms in a local casino-hotel. The room I chose was labeled Lakeside Congregation, the same name as one of our area's Kingdom Hall locations. Gentlemen in suits and ties served as greeters. One of them handed me two small printed pages containing songs to be sung during what was billed as The Memorial for the Lord's Evening Meal. After identifying myself as a visiting writer with questions about Heaven, I took a seat in the back row.

At the front were two tall urns holding palm fronds, and to one side atop a table, one gently curving strand of fuchsia-colored orchid blooms, my mother's favorite potted flower. All the presenters were men and all wore suits and ties. The audience was dressed in a mix of modern attire—suits, skirts, trousers, shirts, sweaters—with the middle-aged and older people tucked more carefully into their garments than the younger ones. They called each other "brother" and "sister," as in Brother Robards, the gentleman who answered some of my questions before and after the event, and Sister Frances, who gave me her phone number so I could call her later.

The service opened with a song, after which the speaker told those gathered that this was "the single most important day of 2011. We're here to commemorate the death of the most important man who ever lived."

I found the service unremittingly Bible-centric. Various men were called to the front to read Bible passages or speak a prayer. The men stepped to the lectern and read passages from Revelation, James, John, Peter, Romans, Isaiah, Matthew, I Corinthians, Hebrews, and Acts, providing explanations for each of them, with emphasis on how believers of "The Truth" would eventually reside with God in the New Heaven, or else on the New Earth (when Jesus returns for the faithful). One speaker explained that mankind received sin from Adam and Eve, that Adam lost his perfect life due to sinning, which relegates all of his offspring to the status of sinners too. All prayers were spoken aloud by the presenters; none by the total congregation.

Unleavened bread and red wine were brought before those gathered, in what was called a "pattern" of the Lord's Evening Meal. One of the presenters explained that only *anointed ones* would partake of the "emblems" (bread and wine), while others "observe with appreciation" as the emblems passed from each person to the next. The non-partakers were the respectful "other sheep" of the flock. Because leavening represents sinfulness, unleavened bread is used to suggest the sinless body and instead of grape juice, fermented red wine is used because it most closely resembles blood poured out in sacrifice. These provide the basis of the covenant for forgiveness of sins. The emblems passed between people, all ethnicities, young and old, in the same manner.

The service incorporated many references to *hope*, as provided through Jesus having died for mankind, through prayer, and the Lord's Evening Meal. There were also many references to "sheep" and "the flock."

One speaker encouraged those gathered to "work toward baptism, remain faithful," and attend meetings.
"For those who are qualified," he said, "engage in
preaching work," and share in the ministry. "Free, personal Bible studies at a time and place convenient to
you" were offered. I learned afterwards that the local
organization also conducts meetings in American Sign
Language, Chinese, and Spanish. No collection plates
were passed, but in the back of the room sat a portable
donation box defended by a large man in a suit.

As the service concluded, Sister Frances, a Latina
with sun-streaked hair, turned to me with a warm smile.
She asked whether I had any questions. The feminist in
me had noticed the dearth of women presenting prayers
or addressing the audience. She allowed that that was
the case, and explained that women are involved in all
other aspects of worship. "A woman baked the unleavened bread," she said. "An honor."

Afterwards, I visited with Brother Robards, a distin-
guished-looking older man with closely shorn white
hair, a soft voice, and a gentle gaze. Two other Brothers
chimed in at times, one whose name I've lost, and another who introduced himself as Brother Kelly. Brother
Robards had earlier explained to me that 144,000 individuals will ascend to Heaven. "They know who they
are," he said, because they've been called personally. He
himself has not been called, so he will hope for "everlasting life on Earth." This will follow from knowing
"The Truth" and being called back to Earth at the conclusion of this "end time" we are currently in. The exact
number of chosen and the reference to "end time" derive from Biblical teachings.

I asked Brother Robards what this form of believing contributes to his life. "It gives me hope," he said, "that the destructive path mankind is on will be reversed." He continued. "It's obvious that man is on the wrong path, ignoring the need for direction from the creator." He told me that he became a Jehovah's Witness at about twelve months old because his mother "knew The Truth." I asked about the role of women in the organization. He explained that the Bible says, "Women will be silent in church." That's why they don't lead.

He had given me a small book titled *WHAT DOES THE BIBLE Really TEACH?* The book appears to be an illustrated tract providing interpretations of Biblical entreaties set in layman's language. One section subtitled "A Model for Husbands" highlights various Biblical quotes, including that women are "the weaker vessel" and that husbands should treat them with the same bodily considerations they show themselves. Under the section "An Example for Wives" I read, "A family is an organization, and to operate smoothly, it needs a head. Even Jesus has One he submits to as his Head. 'The head of the Christ is God,' just as 'the head of a woman is the man.' (Corinthians 11:3)" The passage recommends a wife display a quiet, mild spirit and not try to overtake headship of the family. That same section notes that when a husband makes a final decision that is not in conflict with God's law, the wife shows subjection by supporting it. It gave citations of Acts 5:29 and Ephesians 5:24.

From a table displaying various handouts and small Bibles bound in black, Brother Kelly offered me a book titled *New World Translation of the Holy Scriptures*, which contains cross-references to other related scriptures throughout its pages. One of the other Brothers explained that the Witnesses closely follow the Bible and consider it inspired by God. Roughly forty disciples and followers set it down in words after Jesus's death. In this Bible's foreword, it calls "Jehovah/God the heavenly Author of this sacred library of sixty-six books that holy men from long ago were inspired to write down for our benefit today."

I asked how many versions of the Bible might exist. Brother Robards thought perhaps hundreds. Brother Kelly interjected, "And all of them are accurate because they're based on the word of God."

I asked if that included Islam's sacred text, based as it is on ancient biblical teachings.

Brother Robards broke in. "No."

Me again, the pushy one: "But doesn't it derive from the Old Testament?"

He said Islam is not as "right" as Christianity because it sprang from different descendents of Abraham.

The Bible I was given lists over 165 million copies printed in fifty-nine languages, plus Braille editions, plus video editions of translated portions recited in sign language. This organization takes its missionary work seriously.

Before I exited, Brother Robards introduced to me his wife Donna, she of silver hair and a quiet manner. We shook hands all around before they left, then I asked one of the other Brothers whether the organization's membership had changed over time. He told me that a projected five thousand people would meet at the end of May in Sacramento. In past times tens-of-thousands met at the Cow Palace in San Francisco, but that part of town is "not so good" any longer. He cited a recent television report by Diane Sawyer of ABC News about Jehovah's Witnesses growing the fastest of all religions, at 4.4% per year. According to this Brother, Witnesses keep an annual record and would likely credit a 2.2% growth. Worldwide each week they baptize five thousand people into the faith.

A month later I ended up on a city street behind a Jaguar with license plates that read HVNBOUN. The driver was either one of the 144,000 *chosen*, and knew it, or a different type of believer altogether. That same day, ABC News reported that in one of their polls, three-quarters of Americans believe in an afterlife.

My brief experience with Jehovah's Witnesses brings to mind a book that addresses itself to the ancient history of the Near and Middle East in the millennia before and leading up to Jesus's time, and particularly early records of how and what people worshipped before Christianity arose. Deities were primarily gods and goddesses, a form of nature-worship, useful for explaining or attempting to influence the benevolence of the sun, rain, and aspects of fertility—human and otherwise.

The volume, *When God was a Woman*, may have seemed a revolutionary feminist tract when first published in 1976, though it mainly catalogues and details scholarly and scientific findings about the culture of ancient female-dominated religions and compares them to the development of male-dominated Christianity. Its author, Merlin Stone, points out contradictions, draws parallels, and provides a cultural context for the emergence of Christianity as we know it. She dissects the "myth" of the Garden of Eden and what appear to be appropriations of components from goddess worship recast as aspersions upon biblical female characters so that those prior belief systems could be forced out of popular practice. Stone concludes that various conquerors needed to usurp the authority of matriarchal and matrilineal customs to satisfy the desires of their own patriarchal, patrilineal traditions, in the process demonizing female figures through carefully crafted and edited texts inserted into early editions of the Christian Bible.

On a different note, the British royal wedding of 2011 set me thinking about royalty in relation to religion. If ancient monarchs had promised their subjects and conquered peoples that believing in and honoring *mortal rulers* would at the end of days deliver believers to Heaven and grant them everlasting life, those monarchs could have usurped organized religions' promise of such rewards. Heaven could have been the payoff for timely remittance of taxes and the veneration of self-appointed kings, queens, and emperors. Instead of religious hierarchies being separate from or perhaps beyond the reach of royalty, said rulers might have usurped the spiritual authority eventually claimed by clergy.

18

This Might be Hell

Here is what June W says about Heaven: There is none. "The afterlife is a positive energy, like a force that leaves your body. It's not like the Heaven and Hell thing." Once you go there, you don't want to leave it.

June did at one time believe in Heaven, back when she attended Catholic school, which she describes as being "like total brainwashing." Also "fear-based." The end goal was to avoid burning in Hell, and the daily goal was to avoid getting into trouble. In those early years she had a "neurotic fear of Hell" and a desire to go to Heaven, or at least to purgatory, the interim level preceding Heaven. This made her afraid of death because she didn't know where she would end up and she skipped attending church for years.

Catholic school kids were taught that French kissing was a mortal sin. She shakes her head, her silver hair falling like water around her face as she says that a student she once knew was impregnated by a priest, just another in a list of disenchantments, which includes the Church's discounting of her favorite saint, St. Christopher. She began to challenge Catholic teachings when she was seventeen or eighteen years old. It didn't help that one of her cousins likened the Church to the mafia for extorting money through threats of Hell and promises of protection from Hell in exchange for membership.

Later, June dated an engineer who traveled to Mexico where he observed poor Mexican parents giving money to the Church when their children went without shoes. She also dated Jewish men. "They don't have the Heaven and Hell approach. They have the approach to live right now." Jews, she says, live with less guilt and are "warmer." She would have converted to Judaism had she really loved a Jew. In any case, she broke with the Catholic Church.

June believes in a creator, whom she doesn't call God because that term is too closely aligned with organized religion. There is a higher power, though. And positive energy attracts positive energy, so she's been working on developing that aspect of her awareness along with studying alternative healing techniques and seeking other paths to spirituality.

She is no longer afraid of death, but afraid of suffering, of not being able to take care of herself. She disbelieves that there will be punishment in the afterlife. "The Hell part is right here...If the end came tomorrow, I'd be ready to go." Besides, the afterlife is peaceful. It will be "a large bunch of positive energy orbs...not sight, but feelings."

June's comments point me to a passage that my Christian Science connection quoted from *Science & Health*, their volume of teachings:

> Heaven is not a locality, but a divine state of mind in which all the manifestations of mind are harmonious and immortal, because sin is not there and man is found having no righteousness

of his own, but in possession of the 'mind of the Lord' as the scripture says.

When I ask June for the purpose behind thinking anything comes next, she gestures to the shop around us, her wave taking in the other people sitting at square tables, the counter staff, the insulated dispensers of milk and cream. "People," she says, "want to believe in something that comes after this."

19
The Rapture, Postponed

I n May of 2011 there came what seemed an onslaught of national media coverage about one
California priest of a multi-million-dollar radio
ministry who projected May 21st as the official day of The
Rapture (itself a modern term). The universe would end
with a roar, earthquakes would split the planet and believers would be called to Heaven. Undeterred, I filled
my travel mug with tea and set out for the rural northern California town of Susanville.

It was the type of outing that burnishes burrs from
any stress I've been feeling, the transit from high mountain desert to high mountain ranchlands, dusty tans and
sage greens yielding to forested peaks. To the east, the
shimmer known as Honey Lake, and a crisp spring day
seemingly richer than the sum of its parts—oxygen, hy-
drogen, carbon—in a transparent elixir shot through
with ultraviolet light, fueling my joy, the gathering
clouds, and a car speeding me to my first ever powwow.

In the car's trunk, my early-morning purchase of five
lengths of vintage cotton fabric, the remainders of 1940s
housedresses and quilts. At an estate sale I had browsed
mostly kitchen items and a few truly old things before
finding a box of textiles that included an unfinished
handmade apron and two never-used pillowslips deco-
rated with puppies. Being a sucker for such goods I lift-

ed everything out to find that bundled with the fabrics was a yellowed slice of *The Los Angeles Times* dated Saturday, November 2, 1946. Along with headlines such as "College Expansion Plans Approved," "Pasadena Official Pleads Guilty to Drunk Driving," "Our Lost Opportunity," and "Cornero's Hand Called in Poker Club Suit," was this in capital letters: "FIFTY RELIGIOUS GROUPS TABULATED AT GLENDALE." The story cites:

> More than 54 different churches or denominational groups are represented among Glendale's 99,000 population. A total of 22,700 homes took part in the survey, which was conducted by field workers from 35 cooperating churches. The count provided: Methodists, 2955; Catholics, 2892; Presbyterians, 2115; Baptists, 1602; Christian Scientists, 1040; Lutherans, 991; Episcopalians, 966, Congregationalists, 615; Christians (disciples), 519; Seventh Day Adventists, 386; Mormons, 252; Brethren, 209; Jewish, 169; church of Christ, 112; and Christian Missionary Alliance, 103.

Forty other churches or groups each had fewer than one hundred families represented. It seemed that even across time and space, churches and religions were signaling a desire to be counted.

At the powwow: dozens of dancers and drummers from Paiute and Shoshone and other tribes, elders, parents, teens and children, and folks like me who were there to watch and appreciate. Beyond the community college the mountains stood still while inside the gymnasium the air trembled with drumming and song, drawing fancy dancers, shell dancers, young warriors, and others into the ring. I dined on an Indian taco and browsed the craft booths, eventually driving home in the late afternoon, arriving back in Reno approximately two hours after the world did not end.

A few days later, a Christian friend marveled at the audacity of the preacher who had built a well-funded church upon predictions of an elusive Rapture (this was his second failure and counting). She thought that such prophesies might be explained by mental illness, that throughout time there have been so many warnings which have proven unfounded. The curious thing, we agreed, is that some modern so-called prophets actually believe what they predict. Others don't, of course. They simply see an opportunity to further their own notoriety, or pad their pocketbooks at the expense of the hopeful, who drain their savings in pursuit of a seat when the music stops.

May's Rapture did not arrive, so the good Reverend did what any salesman worth his salt would do—he adjusted his pitch and shifted the delivery date out a bit, this time to October 21, 2011. Everyone I know, Christian and non-, had pursued their usual activities on May 21: mowing the lawn, preparing for the coming week of school, those ordinary things that fill up one's weekend. Folks who had invested their life savings to help finance the Reverend must have stood blinking in the next morning's light, wondering just what had gone wrong.

One Saturday morning soon thereafter, I stuffed a few dollars into my pocket and pulled on a baseball cap. I'm partial to certain kinds of old books. To find them within my budget I scout estate sales and yard sales.

On a narrow street in a neighborhood adjacent to Virginia Lake Park, I pulled over for a jumbled display of sale items and there encountered the man of the house, a clean-shaven fellow of sixty-something. He followed me about while I perused the tables of goods, talking at me like someone craving conversation. First he bewailed the shoppers who don't appreciate the intrinsic value of the kinds of items he had set out: dolls, glassware, candlesticks, knickknacks. Young people's heads, he said, are turned by liberal teachers who fill their brains with nonsense. They think that life is all about talking on the phone and texting, and they want everything easy, want immediate gratification. I gathered from his lamentations that young people rarely buy used dolls, glassware, candlesticks, or other knickknacks.

I could have wished for a shoehorn to get a word in. The man's commentary ranged from a narrative about driving from San Francisco to Reno in a 1967 Chevy with a sixteen-gallon gas tank, to the Federal government meddling in the price of gas by applying forty-three cents per gallon in taxes. Gasoline had gotten ridiculously expensive (those damn taxes). And if a person read the Constitution they could see that this country was founded on "In God We Trust."

That's when I told him I don't believe in God and I'd just as soon eliminate God references from U.S. currency and other places related to government. Amazingly, he did not fault my position, perhaps because he wanted a listener for his anecdotes and complaints. When he began ranting about the "damn liberals running the government" being the ruin of things via "ObamaCare," I challenged him to voice support of Bush-era policies which enabled oil companies to post billions of dollars in 2010 profits; so much for the cost of gasoline. I also expressed my disappointment about all the casualties sustained in the Iraq war, which had been founded on a Bush-era reading of misinformation. That was roughly the point at which he began to froth. "Are you a liberal?" he asked, a look of horror on his face.

More like a cross between liberal and independent, or perhaps I'd qualify as a progressive, but it seemed easier to nod in response and see how he'd react.

"Oh," he said. "Then your mind is closed. The liberals would have us all go back to living in log cabins. God made this earth and all its resources, so why wouldn't we use them?" At that point he followed me to my car where I planned to seek refuge. "Okay," he added, "you don't buy that part. But the whole liberal government has ruined things." He said something about the need to shrink government social programs and subsidies; the time had come to slash and burn them all.

I held my open car door like a shield between us as I asked whether he received Social Security benefits. I proposed he refuse them, or send them back and thereby help slash government spending through reducing the payouts of entitlement programs.

He sputtered and waved his hands, but to his credit he didn't touch my car or reach for me. "I earned those," he shouted. "Those are mine, I earned those."

I climbed into my car, started it, and pulled carefully away from the curb. As is often the case, two minutes later I thought of a question I should have asked. I did not have it in me to backtrack to the tables filled with dozens of items waiting for purchasers, but it crossed my mind to wonder whether that particular believer had waited on May 21st for a Rapture gone missing.

20

A Hundred Billion Billion Stars

F riends know me as someone who loves the Oregon coast. Must be something about its raw nature, the midnight broom clinging to sheer roadside cliffs, the foxglove and cowslip parsley sprung up in grassy swales fed by surface water. Views of the ocean stretch toward places I'll never see, strings of pelicans patrol the beaches, and house-sized boulders perch in the tidal zone. At the shoreline: the constant churn of sand and foam, novel life-forms catching in pools of sloshy broth. I have lived so long in the high desert that all watery things exert a pull on me.

In mid-June I drove with my husband on I-97, heading north past Upper Klamath Lake, when to our right came into view a little bit of roadside marketing for God—a boarded-up cabin set among tall and waving grasses. To its front porch was nailed a yellow sign with black lettering: "Believe in the Lord and you will be saved." Thirty minutes later, on the approach to Crater Lake, a song by one of my favorite 1960s groups came on the radio—"Jesus is Just Alright" by the Doobie Brothers. Some songs are great for a sing-along , and that's one of them.

As you might imagine, when a writer is working on a project with a specific theme, not only do they see that theme manifested in ever-increasing ways about them, but friends suggest books and articles that touch on or near the topic at hand. I've been lucky in that regard because it would not be possible to read more than a fraction of what has been written on the subject of churches, or Christianity, or God-belief. Luckily, though, I've encountered a number of published treatments of those subjects. Some I clipped and saved in a file because I was planning my upcoming research and trying to flesh out my novel's female protagonist, someone knowledgeable about churches and faith. Other articles and books appeared in my viewfinder, unbidden but welcome.

Kim B lent me a paper published in 1940 which had belonged to her father. "Theodicy for Non-Majors in Philosophy," was authored by Lawrence J. Heney, S.J., Ph.D., chairman of the philosophy department of Loyola University of Los Angeles, a Catholic institution "rooted in Jesuit and Marymount traditions." Though *theodicy* derives from "divine justice" and my Webster's gives the definition "...defense of God's goodness and omnipotence in view of the existence of evil," Heney's introduction suggests that theodicy is the study of why, as opposed to how, the universe exists. On yellowing pages, the 8-1/2 x 11-inch bound text runs 124 pages.

I really did try to slog my way through the twenty-two theses and their "proofs," eventually growing accustomed to the warped visual effect of wavering keystrikes and the quaint charm of uncorrected errors. I have an old R.L. Smith Corona that might be from that same era and can picture the Philosophy department secretary squinting at Dr. Heney's scritch-scratchy writing as she hammered through sandwiched layers of bond and carbon paper. No cut and paste, or computer formatting. More likely she—undoubtedly a *she*—typed a new draft each time the author desired yet more edits.

Heney's theses include proving God's existence through "a posteriori" (inductive) versus "a priori" (deductive) reasoning; The Absolutely Necessary Being is a Personal God; The Innate Desire of Man for Perfect Happiness Proves the Existence of God; The Existence of Some Mighty Intelligence is Proved From The Order of the Universe, This Intelligence is God; God Most Perfectly Knows Himself and All Else that is Knowable; and others that assert God's immensity. Each thesis seems to offer proof through a vigorous assertion of the thesis itself.

Additionally, the author proposes that "Speculative Atheism and Agnosticism are Absurd and Most Detrimental to the Human Race." In Chapter Five he writes, "The errors of Atheism and Agnosticism are refuted with no great difficulty, since both are contrary to right reason." He summarizes various "modern" attitudes toward God, which are in opposition to "rational proofs" and "scholastic" thought." I gave up at that point, but the author gets my nod for attempting to argue his position by writing like a true believer.

Notwithstanding her father's religious studies, and in spite of finding Christmas music "uplifting and beautiful," Kim is a self-identified *agneist*, some days agnostic, other days full-on atheist. She's the one person I know to claim that "religious people have it easy" through their monopoly of our culture's useful, rich-sounding sayings. To wit: It's almost universally American to offer "Bless you" in response to someone's sneeze. There is no good substitution, says Kim, though being of German heritage she might proffer "gesundheit." She prefers the warmer sentiment "Bless you," but feels awkward using language once meant to invoke God's protection in keeping a sneezer's spirit from abandoning his body. She laments that other phrases pale by comparison. With a wag of her head and a glance into the middle distance she intones the language for an imaginary sympathy card, "'Sending positive thoughts your way.' How lame is that?"

I have a fortune from a cookie that came with an order of Chinese takeout. It reads "A new relationship is about to blossom. You will be blessed." Where do such cookies and their fortunes come from? For all I know they're manufactured in Hoboken, though we think of them as crossing the oceans to get here. I think of word blessings coming from any number of sources, and physical blessings as gifts from nature.

To revisit gesundheit: It derives from "health-hood," a sensible, thoughtful response since it bids the recipient good health. Kim, though, says we need to develop and launch a few appropriate secular phrases instead of bastardizing religious language. That woman. She's a stickler for propriety.

A man I have known for twenty-five years was preparing a bedroom door for installation in my house. His sister is a born-again fundamentalist. Her interjections of religious references into virtually every conversation they have are "getting a little old." When I asked what he believes about an afterlife, he said he wants to believe something will come next. Also, he notes that our universe is more magnificent than he can credit to natural laws. Something, some creator, must have started the ball rolling, begetting our universe along with what appear to be multiple universes.

He asked me what I believe happens when a person dies. I said, "You're gone." He gave that some thought while sanding the edge of a pine door before saying he hopes there is more to it.

In an on-line article titled "Does the Universe Need God?" Sean Carroll, of the California Institute of Technology, explains the concept of "multi-verses." The current science of cosmology can account for not just the universe we live within, but will eventually explain a universe with different regions, some "outside our observable horizon" in which conditions are very different from the constants we live with, including laws governing physics. He notes that our human understanding of universal cogs and energy and space-time evolves every year to include yet more aspects previously imagined but not proven. In the observable universe there are a hundred billion galaxies, each containing a hundred billion stars like those in our Milky Way, which is thought to contain two hundred billion. Science now understands that space and time are dynamic, changing in response to energy and matter.

Though I can barely wrap my mind around the concepts of nuclear fusion, dark energy, and vacuum energy (let's not even attempt string theory), that doesn't mean I need dismiss them. Carroll cites various arguments in favor of and against natural laws as eventual explanation for cosmological discoveries. He notes that some people favoring a creator offer what he identifies as a "meta-explanation" or "meta-explanatory" account, a claim that because something happens there must also be an explanation for why it happens. He grants that it's nice to provide reasons for why something "is the case," and reminds readers that early explorers and scientists did not uncover within their lifetimes every possible answer for the natural phenomena they observed; likewise, we do not have all the answers for the universe/multi-verse (at least we don't have them *yet*). Carroll writes:

> Why are some people so convinced of the need for a meta-explanatory account, while others are perfectly happy without one? I would suggest that the impetus to provide such an account comes from our experiences within the world, while the suspicion that there is no need comes from treating the entire universe as something unique, something for which a different set of standards is appropriate.

The man sanding doors did not write this next "PostSecret" but he might agree with it: *I long for something I can't understand and sometimes I feel like it will never come and then I get scared that this is all there is.*

21

The Mind of the Beholder

I have lately been rereading portions of *The Poisonwood Bible*, Barbara Kingsolver's epic story about an American missionary family in postcolonial Belgian Congo. The novel's family faces a clash of cultures and ultimately loses its father to his own descent into madness. These are fictional characters, of course, but good fiction conveys truths about the human condition and the world around us. In this novel a family faces many obstacles to survival in a wild and foreign country, carrying with them years of memorized Bible lessons that provide scant aid in quieting the rumblings of their empty stomachs, forestalling a stalking leopard, or saving any living creature from the onslaught of carnivorous driver ants. Years later, even family members who disbelieved continued justifying and trying to comprehend their father's religious fervor.

The story renders a universal truth about how we forever carry early family lessons, whether unconditionally loving, instructional, abusive, or religious. Even if we compartmentalize or disavow or dismiss what those experiences represent, somehow we become a vessel for bearing them into the future. I am certain that is why I could sketch a reasonably accurate diagram of the church sanctuary where I sat with my mother those many Sundays ago. The same for the living room of our house on 66th Avenue, and the public pool where I took lifesaving lessons in a brown and yellow two-piece swimsuit. I could reconstruct a particular casserole which was a family favorite, and navigate the winding route to high school in a city where I haven't lived for forty years. Minutia, the inevitable, necessary building blocks of a life.

I've been trying to piece together how humans have carried into modern times so many religious traditions grounded in ancient theologies. A July 2011 ABC News investigation into reports of what are known as Marion sightings (sightings of the Virgin Mary) also made mention of brain science. One expert shown on camera said, "There are differences in the brains of believers versus non-believers," without illuminating what specific differences—physical or operational?—have been found, while suggesting that a predisposition to religious belief may be "hardwired." I knew instantly that I must seek out more on the subject.

Also in July came a weekly newspaper column posing the question: "How will God treat nonbelievers?" One answer came from a local professor of philosophy and religion, William Tell Gifford:

> When believers judge others negatively for their disbeliefs, the whole concept of belief becomes troublesome. The problem hinges on the mistaken assumption that we choose our beliefs. Believers who suppose that an atheist can choose to believe in God or the atheist who claims that believers choose to believe in God, show a lack of reflection on this problem. Imagine asking the same people if they could will themselves to believe in the existence of flesh-and-blood unicorns, or if they could

stop believing in the planet Neptune, which can't be seen with the naked eye, anyway. It quickly becomes obvious that we can't just will a belief into being. The genesis or transformation of a belief is complicated by incalculable variables. Although choice may be part of the equation in the formation of a belief, the idea that choice is the sole or primary driver is naïve and presumptuous.

Though I describe disbelief as natural to me, I had not previously considered that believers might have less than 100% choice in matters of belief. That while under the influence of familial bonds and the culture around them they somehow remain blind to the machinations of religion.

In his book THE BLIND WATCHMAKER—WHY THE EVIDENCE OF EVOLUTION REVEALS A UNIVERSE WITHOUT DESIGN, evolutionary biologist Richard Dawkins explained natural selection, its effects on future generations, and the resulting morphology of offspring. Dominant genetic patterns create a favored climate for an organism's development. Could it be then that dominant patterns of thought and behavior *surrounding* a person, bombarding a person, during emotional and intellectual development might influence that person's later thoughts and behaviors?

I have long maintained that we are *consumers* of other people's formal and informal communications. Add to that all the advertising, political rhetoric, entertainment, and music that reaches us on any given day. Even when we think we're above the clamor or tuning it out, or in disagreement, lots of it sticks. Bits, maybe buckets-full become lodged in our memories, so that even if we don't espouse the same views or tastes advocated by the onslaught of messages, we contain references to them. If it's in our brain, it's a part of us, yes? We are each a product of that which we brought to the light of day and all we've encountered since.

Throughout these past years I have, perhaps unfairly, considered God-believers somehow deficient when it comes to rational thought. Before you think me cruel, let me explain that I don't mean IQ; I mean critical thinking, the type of thought that shapes the sciences and mathematics. I saw God-belief as driven by emotion and emotional needs, either arising spontaneously from some internal place or induced by exposure to outside influences. Or both. And yet, what does that perspective suggest about scientists, academics, scholars, and astronomers, extraordinary thinkers all, who believe in God or gods? And how to account for the millions of believers worldwide? I couldn't.

Then I read a work of non-fiction that set bells chiming: *The Believing Brain—From Ghosts and Gods to Politics and Conspiracies—How We Construct Beliefs and Reinforce Them as Truths*, by Michael Shermer, a developmental psychologist and author who has for decades studied the human brain's formation of beliefs (not only religious beliefs; also social, economic, and political) and the many biases we employ to support them. Oh, the biases (he enumerates twenty-five)!

Shermer argues that our brains are *belief engines*, discerning patterns in virtually everything, patterns that in earliest human development led to survival through correct interpretation of environmental risks but also through errors that favored safety (as in fleeing a predator when the potential threat was in fact only wind rustling grasses). Natural selection favored those who remained safe, including those who had fled in error. Thus, through evolution, human brains developed what he calls *patternicity*, the tendency to see patterns in almost everything, and *agenticity*, the tendency to assign knowing agents for those patterns.

His thesis is that over many millennia, human brains have become wired to form beliefs then seek explanation and substantiation for them. The end result is that humans naturally develop all manner of beliefs that are unsupportable by empirical evidence. This tendency, says Shermer, is natural. I understand him to argue that for a majority of people, subconscious pattern identification and substantiation function like elements of a default setting. This default, unlike with, say, personal computers, cannot easily be reset, and over time has influenced the human genome.

Furthermore, Shermer's research, including studies of twins and fMRI studies conducted by other scientists, attributes just over 50% of the origins of religious beliefs to genetics and roughly 40% to cultural influences such as family, friends, and church.

It seems to me that even if the earliest tendencies toward pattern recognition were inadvertent (perhaps a matter of probability),the resulting survival skills must have become reinforced behaviors. In that case, other survival behaviors could influence brain evolution too, could they not? How about the myriad instances of people being forced or coerced into practicing belief systems thrust upon them by conquerors or others in control? Might the perpetual adoption of ideologies or theologies for self preservation, or to keep one's kinfolk alive, over time affect the brain's evolution? Such sur-

vival strategies go back as far as there have been bands
of people conquered by others. And might coerced ritual
behavior create a self-perpetuating feedback loop? I'm
thinking here of religious requirements delivered by the
pointed ends of swords. And if belief in the supernatural
was at one time useful for making order from, or trying
to influence, the natural world, perhaps a tendency toward belief in the supernatural became ingrained in the
human psyche.

I myself have not circumnavigated the globe, don't
possess empirical evidence of its marble-like shape, but
I accept the facts provided by others. You could say I
take them on faith. I turn to others as well for explanations of the universe's working parts and particles, and
trust the modern scientific vetting process. There are
gaps and holes (of course!) because we will likely never
peel back the final sweating layer to get at the nugget of
our existence. I sleep perfectly well, thank you, in spite
of the gaps and holes, though others may need to fill
them with remnants of those early patterns and agents,
seasoned perhaps with elements derived from myth and
magic.

Which leads to this question: When industry, medicine, science, and language are ever-malleable and
evolving, why do people cling to millennia-old systems
of belief? Looking back through time, most religions
appear to have cribbed the attributes of prior gods, goddesses, and supernatural beings, one civilization's deities begetting those of the next, like so many dominoes
of imagination and emotion falling forward into time to
soothe the need for order and salve the current era's ills
and discontents. An old practice, and modern too, the
borrowing of another's work to season your own.

One writers' adage goes something like, "Only steal from the best." It acknowledges that the appropriation of a phrase or line or a few bars of melody is bound to happen, is virtually unavoidable because we're all influenced by what we hear and read. If you inject into your own story (or lecture, scripture, essay) a few bits you've stolen and reworked, they become yours. They're *new* when presented in a new context. So it was, and still is, with language, cultural customs, music, and religion. Priestesses appropriating from myths, the priests from the priestesses, the prophets from the priests, the shamans, the wise men, the troubadours, minstrels, folk singers, laymen, writers. There are no original stories, so I've heard, which seems also to apply to religion. New versions of the old stories; new variations on the ancient myths.

While writing this memoir I came to the conclusion that humans have an innate affinity for magic and myth. But if we are to accept Shermer's proposition, such an affinity could in fact be a genetic predisposition that evolved in response to how people once addressed their knowledge deficits and soothed their fears.

I own a volume on mythology that could anchor a rowboat, such is the lengthy record of how humans have embraced gods and goddesses, mystics, and of course magic, the honey of our sweetest dreams. Where once there were early goddesses of the Middle Kingdom, Greek and Roman gods, sacrificial rites, elaborate religious and pagan ceremonies, pyramids and elaborate crypts, there are now other superheroes and heroines: Superman and Green Hornet, Cat Woman, X-Men and Avengers. Sleeping Beauty, fairy godmothers, the Tooth

Fairy. Peter Pan. Lord of the Rings. Vampires. And of course, Harry Potter!

If myths are traditional stories containing super human beings, stories passed down through the ages, perhaps the Potter gang will someday be viewed as 21st century myths. Have any other fantasy characters gained as large a following? Only might the sum of all past fictional children's characters eclipse the many readers of Potter. The stories, the movies, the merchandise. Pottermania has approached religiosity by adherents who adore its fantastical characters, possessors of super powers who arrived ... how exactly? From the mating of humans and magical beings? The kicker: They fight evil forces and perform deeds that resemble miracles.

While consuming these stories, readers and watchers become transported through a temporary belief in a parallel reality; the outside *real* world is left behind while they enjoin the inside *fictional* world. What should we make of such human fascination and attraction to eye-of-newt tales? It seems that human imagination gravitates to, perhaps thrives upon, escapism through fantasy.

So now I'm wondering: In the aftermath of the Harry Potter craze, will the percentage of God-believers tick upward? Will those revelers of JK Rowling's magical world become followers of one of the thousands of extant religions? On the other end of the continuum, though, is the modern embrace of reality television and a growing readership for memoirs. Do those trends signal a drift away from fantasy toward warts-and-all, stub-your-toe realism?

We learn more each year about life forms of the deep ocean, the time-space continuum, subatomic particles, dark matter, and the early evolution of Homo sapiens. Each year, scientists utilize intelligence, creativity, precision instruments, and perseverance to solve what were once mysteries about life on this planet. To me those pursuits seem grand enough to rival any allure of myth and magic.

Numerous are the different God-believing religions, reflecting characteristics unique to specific cultures, communities, and spiritual leaders, with diverse views about the origin of the gospels, how to interpret Biblical passages, and whether to view the Bible's narrative literally or figuratively, or a combination thereof. They differ widely about women's roles in worship services, about sexual orientation, and about non-believers. At the same time, individuals the world over continue to shape and mold their worship habits to fit their own changing needs. Perhaps we are entering a time when God-belief will metamorphose from its current form(s) into something bearing a new outline and texture, while scientific discoveries emerge to address the remaining mysteries of the human organism and its appetites and dreams.

I am greatly relieved by Shermer's theory of how beliefs develop, since it posits that half the reason for God-belief may be attributed to primal instinct at work. As hard as it has been for me to fathom God-belief, it must be equally difficult for believers to understand just what makes atheists so, shall we say, *dense* about beliefs which well up naturally in others. A mutually wide chasm divides us.

For what it's worth, when I reached the end of Shermer's book I felt myself softening toward believers everywhere, and adjusting some of my earlier suppositions. I am beginning to buy into the notion that my own disbelief may well be the inevitable byproduct of a believing mother mated to a disbelieving father, the result of which is zero genetic coding for a predisposition to God-belief. Other people, perhaps many millions of current believers, contain coding for a predisposition toward belief, which might bloom in response to emotions, family and cultural influences and/or an affinity for myth and magic (perhaps also genetically coded). As a result, I'm feeling clearer-eyed about believers doing what they do.

In case you are wondering whether my church and synagogue visits awakened me to a personal religious truth heretofore unrecognized ... they did not, in part because my mind distinguishes *believing* from *knowing*, with religious faith, God-belief in particular, a type of unrequited believing. No proof, no pudding. There was a time when I tested how it felt to wear the mantle of agnosticism (the term *agnostic shuffle* comes to mind). I could not subscribe to a Christian theology or give credence to a creator-figure, but I wasn't then as certain as I have since become about what it is to disbelieve. The thing was, I did not yearn for any super-being to fill the gaps in what I did not know, someone grander than the astronomers and scientists, the physicians and philosophers of the world.

Believers will say that they *know* there is a God, they feel him, they love him, they need no other proof than the world's splendor and its disasters, human and otherwise; all are proof of God at work. They say they know, but actually, they *believe*, which as I see it is a step removed from knowing, an internalization meant to fulfill a purpose that is not the purpose of knowing. While that seems enough for millions of people, it is insufficient for me. In spite of a year's exposure to churches and their followers, my worldview remains this: We are on this planet with no God. You, me, and everyone else, a meadowlark, and the infinite night sky.

There are many people with worldviews similar to mine, probably more than anyone has accurately counted. Not that you would recognize any of us by our thoughts, which whirl 'round in hidden places, but you might peg some of us by our non-conformist ways. We might be that person in church who doesn't sing along, or the one *not* in church but home watching sports, or organizing a food drive, running a marathon, running a company, or a country ... you get the idea.

September 23, 2011 ~

Driving to an evening with friends, I follow McCarran Boulevard to Peckham Lane where I end up in an adjacent lane to a red Toyota 4-Runner, its tailgate and the white camper shell pasted with messages calling for attention: "Trust Jesus" and "Believe or Be Left." In shoe polish on the passenger side panel were three references to gospel chapters and verses.

Believers might know these verses by heart; just noting the references might bring to mind their phrasing, and perhaps the circumstances under which they are commonly used. To look them up I go to one of four Bibles in our household library: A *Red Letter Edition and Cyclopedic Masonic Bible* (my husband's, inherited from his father), a *Strong's Concordance of the Holy Bible* (purchased by me at an estate sale), an illustrated *Bible for the Young and Fireside Commentator* (missing half its cover), and my husband's *Holy Bible* from 1956. The latter provides the following for the Toyota's declarations:

For John 3:16:
> For God so loved the world that he gave his only
> Son, that whoever believes in him should not
> perish but have eternal life.

For Acts 2:21:
> And it shall be that whoever calls on the name of
> the Lord shall be saved.

For Acts 10:43:
> To him all the prophets bear witness that every
> one who believes in him receives forgiveness of
> sins through his name.

The license plate on this rig was: **John 336** which
reads:
> He who believes in the Son has eternal life; he
> who does not obey the Son shall not see life, but
> the wrath of God rests upon him.

In marketing, the term "vehicle" applies to various
delivery devices for advertisements, promotions, and
public relations messages. Television is a vehicle, as are
mailers, as are town hall meetings. Vehicles deliver. The
truck sporting Christian messages is probably not a local
church's grassroots marketing tool, but a multi-purpose
vehicle—one that carries believers while also promoting
the teachings they believe.

I began this project more than a year ago with the goal
of accomplishing my research and getting a start on a
new novel, with few expectations other than to experience some interesting mornings at church and to har-
vest insights useful for shading fictional characters.

Reflecting now on my descriptions of churches and synagogue, they seem scrupulously objective: the colors, the carpet, the windowless walls. I *was* wearing my researcher's cap—Just the facts, Ma'am. When I sat in church, the view was in large part the backs of people's heads: the bald spots, the tonsures, the teased and over-dyed and slept-in coiffures, the slouch of the sleep-deprived, the fidgeting, the whispered asides. I sat there wishing to see those people's faces, their expressions while praying and singing and soaking up sermons. That is my typical focus—on people—with an appreciation for how their body language and their own words transmit clues to the human condition.

Though the services I observed did not transform me, the preachers each spoke with passion: Pastor Louie, Father Vercellone, all of them. And Rabbi Appleby's approach seemed, well, fresh. But as I wasn't seeking God, it's no surprise I did not find God.

Just because the glow of worship services didn't rub off on me doesn't mean that those places weren't full of earnest people connecting through mutual prayer, the touch of a hand, a knowing gaze, and common beliefs. Observing such diverse congregations inspired me to think more deeply about my own religious history and that of other people. It also made me want to share my journey with readers who might want to figuratively stand in those church doorways, peering in. But you don't have to settle for words on paper. You can make up your own mind about them. You can visit them and see for yourself.

As it turns out I have gained much more than material for my novel, including an expanded perspective about the nature of God-belief, insights into the ways churches market themselves, a sampling of what some folks believe about Heaven, and an appreciation for how believers open the door to strangers, muddy boots and all.

My visits to houses of worship, seasoned by many thought-provoking books, articles, documentaries, lectures, and interviews, have eased my bewilderment about believers. I feel less confounded by so many people the world over embracing God. It now seems to me that they may contain something I do not—an appetite for faith inscribed in evolution's special code. As natural as language, as companionship. As desire.

As a result I'll be more interested than ever to speak with believers, to listen and watch, and to ponder the meaning of it all. There's no off-switch for my curiosity, and that, friends, is as it should be.

Acknowledgements

In addition to the individuals named herein, who shared their beliefs in support of this project, I am grateful and lucky to have had the following people shine their light in my direction: ultimate sounding board and First Reader, Lisa Mortara; readers of early chapters—Alexandria King and a writer named Christine; Jennifer Mannix (you know why); and my ever-patient and supportive friends and family inside whose circle I worked in peace.

To Jim: Howsoever it was that we found each other, I am gladder than you know.

Books Cited and/or Recommended

The Believing Brain—From Ghosts and Gods to Politics and Conspiracies—How We Construct Beliefs and Reinforce Them as Truths (2011) Michael Shermer; Times Books, Henry Holt & Co., LLC

When God was a Woman (1976) Merlin Stone; current edition by Barnes & Noble Books

Buy-ology—Truth and Lies About Why We Buy (2010) Martin Lindstrom; Broadway Books, an imprint of Random House, Inc.

Heaven—Our Enduring Fascination with the Afterlife (2010) Lisa Miller; Harper, a division of HarperCollins

A Lifetime of Secrets (2007) Frank Warren; William Morrow, an imprint of HarperCollins

Good without God—What a Billion Nonreligious People Do Believe (2009) Greg M. Epstein; HarperCollins

The Moral Landscape—How Science Can Determine Human Values (2010) Sam Harris; Free Press

The Blind Watchmaker (1996) Richard Dawkins; W.W. Norton & Company

Misquoting Jesus (2005) Bard D. Ehrman; Harper One, an imprint of HarperCollins

Questions for Discussion

1. For readers who are religious: How did you learn about your religion or set of beliefs? What influences led to your choices?

2. At what age did you first participate in religious activities, and what do you recall thinking about them?

3. For non-believers: Were there religious influences in your life that you understood and rejected? Or, were there no obvious influences pointing you toward a religious belief system?

4. For all readers: Who do you speak with about your beliefs or disbelief? Is it a topic that comes up in casual conversation or only during theological or philosophical debate?

5. How do you view nature? Can a person find God on a mountaintop?

6. Do American religious influences color your language and/or how you think about currency, taking oaths, or the Pledge of Allegiance?

7. For non-believers: Do you find it difficult to identify yourself as an atheist? What terminology do you use?

8. What, if any, correlation do you see between an affinity for myth and magic, and an affinity for God-belief?

9. Is America moving toward organized religion or away from it? Do you endorse "a buffet of choices?"

10. Have you visited temples, churches, or synagogues in order to learn more about how others practice their beliefs? What did you take away from that experience?

11. Do you have ideas for how churches might market themselves? Does the notion of churches as purveyors of services make sense? Does it repel you?

12. Do you feel as if your belief or disbelief is innate or acquired? Does an evolutionary explanation for God-belief (or creator-belief) resonate with you? Furthermore, do you come from a family of believers or non-believers?

Made in the USA
Charleston, SC
22 February 2013